THE
·COOK'S ROOM·

THE
·COOK'S ROOM·
A Celebration of the Heart of the Home

General Editor: Alan Davidson

HarperCollins*Publishers*

THE COOK'S ROOM. Copyright © 1991 by Weldon Russell Pty Ltd/Rosemary Wilkinson. All rights reserved. Printed in Hong Kong. No part of this book may be used or reproduced in any manner whatsoever without written permission except in the case of brief quotations embodied in critical articles and reviews. For information address HarperCollins Publishers, 10 East 53rd Street, New York, NY 10022.

FIRST U.S. EDITION

Produced by Weldon Russell Pty Ltd
in association with Rosemary Wilkinson
4/52 Ourimbah Road
Mosman NSW 2088 Australia

Project director: Rosemary Wilkinson
Picture researcher: Shona Wood
Caption writer: Lynn Humphries
Production: Jane Hazell
Editorial assistant: Margaret Whiskin
Produced by: Mandarin Offset

A KEVIN WELDON PRODUCTION

Library of Congress Cataloging-in-Publication Data

The Cook's room : a celebration of the heart of the home / Alan Davidson, general editor. — 1st U.S. ed.
        p. cm.
    Includes index.
    ISBN 0-06-016645-2
    1. Kitchens. 2. Cookery. I. Davidson, Alan. 1924–
TX653.C88 1991
643'.3—dc20   90-56351

91 92 93 94 95   10 9 8 7 6 5 4 3 2 1

Endpapers: *A variety of ladles and scrubbing brushes ready for use in a kitchen in China.*

Half title page: *The simplicity of this Spanish kitchen is accentuated by the boldly decorated earthenware platters and blue and white tiles.*

Title page: *A pan of oeufs en meurette sits atop a cast-iron range. The term* meurette *is applied to certain dishes cooked in a red wine sauce, a specialty of Burgundy, Bresse, and Dombes in France. The sauce often contains baby onions, bacon, and mushrooms.*

Opposite contents page: *A battery of copper utensils in a Portuguese kitchen. Copper is universally admired as an excellent conductor of heat. It heats up and cools down quickly, making it easier to control the rate of cooking.*

Opposite: *A kamado oven dominates the center of a Japanese kitchen. Steamers and saucepans are set over the holes cut in the top.*

CONTENTS

INTRODUCTION
Alan Davidson ❖ 9

INTRODUCTION

❖

I *suppose that just about all of us have a stereotype of a kitchen stored in our memory, a mental image that flashes up on our internal video screens when the word "kitchen" gives us the necessary prompt. That has certainly been true for me, although I have two stereotypes, and which of them comes up depends on the context. My Scottish grandmother's kitchen appears when the context is completely general, whereas our own kitchen pops up if the context relates to the present time.*

One effect of this book will be to dilute the potency of such stereotypes. The collective impact of these vivid and varied essays is bound to leave us all thinking about "the kitchen" in a rather different way. The effect on me has been a new appreciation of the kitchen as something that echoes and typifies other cultures and other lifestyles, a room (or sometimes a separate building) whose functions always include cooking but may embrace many other activities too.

Most readers of *The Cook's Room* will be accustomed to a kitchen where the cooking is done by members of the family (or other) group who live together. A servant to do the cooking has become a rarity, except for those grand establishments which lie outside the scope of this book. However, since many of the essays, concerned with what is traditional rather than what is current, go back a century or more, the paid cook appears; and, naturally enough, wherever she or he appears (as in the Amsterdam townhouse described by Anneke Ammerlaan, or that "dreadful room" in Whittier where M. F. K. Fisher learned to cook), the kitchen is a different place, and does not fully "belong" to the family in the way with which we are familiar—although the family may regain possession of it on "cook's night out."

From our own experience of inhabiting the British Embassy in Laos, my wife and I know that the kitchen in such an establishment, although legally part of a building which belongs to the British government, is in practice the fiefdom of the cook (and not infrequently of his or her family and friends too), and that a visit to the kitchen must be heralded ahead of time and take place with due formality.

The atmosphere of a kitchen in which there is no paid cook is quite different; yet it may vary so much that one marvels at the ability of that one word, "kitchen," and of its equivalent in other languages, to cover them all. Incidentally, virtually all European words for kitchen come from the Latin verb *coquere*, to cook, and its related nouns.

The exuberance of Provençal design is as colorful as the region's cuisine (previous page). Cooks take advantage of the vast range of quality fruit and vegetables from the Rhône and the Durance valleys—the largest areas of production in France.

This root word was adopted, naturally enough, in the Romance languages; but it also percolated through Old High German into Polish and Russian and then southward again into Bulgarian. It always kept its original meaning; and a kitchen is always where cooking is done, mostly for human beings, but also for animals, as Marie-Noële Denis points out.

A kitchen may be just a kitchen, or it may serve other purposes too. Willie Graham indicates that in the Chesapeake region of Virginia the detached kitchen was "the point of interaction between the blacks and the whites." And in many places, including Alsace, the kitchen was a meeting place for women of the neighborhood as well as of the house.

If there is only one communal room in a dwelling, that room must of course include the functions of kitchen, eating area, and living room. The description by Elisabeth Luard of her Hebridean kitchen provides a lively account of how this works in one setting; and Richard Hosking tells us of the similar arrangement of a small house in the Japanese countryside.

However, a kitchen may also stand in its own right, free of other functions, and it may indeed be the heart of a small empire. Anita Stewart, in her charming essay about kitchens of rural Canada, links it firmly to the kitchen garden and orchard. But the typical empire is an indoor one. Just as cooking calls for subsidiary operations, especially storage, the kitchen may be flanked by its own offshoots, such as what is called a pantry in English. This English word comes from a root which indicates clearly the original purpose of this room, which was to store bread; not even butter to go with bread, since a large house would have both a *paneterie* and a *boterie*. But this original meaning of "pantry" has been extended over the centuries to cover any room, usually adjacent to the kitchen, for storing provisions, including cold meats.

In concert with the introduction of refrigerators and easier shopping for food, the role and size of the pantry have diminished in Europe and North America, especially in urban environments. In all of my parents' successive houses in various English towns in the 1930s and 1940s there was something we called a pantry; and in our own house in London there was a similar place, which we called the "larder," until the 1970s. But all these were really just cupboards, not a whole room—nothing like the magnificent Turkish pantry described by Nevin Halici, Alicia Rios' lovely white-tiled pantry in Spain, or the *bit ala'oula* in Morocco evoked by Jill Tilsley-Benham's poetic prose. Still less did they resemble what we hear about in Julie Sahni's essay on the traditional Raj kitchen in India, which had both an elegant pantry and a large storeroom, and where the pantry provided a meeting ground for mistress and cook.

It is evident from the descriptions of kitchens and pantries and storerooms in different parts of the world that their layout and equipment have been influenced not only by the need (or absence of need) to store food, but also by the nature of local resources. This influence may be detectable as a fundamental feature of kitchen architecture—for example, the importance of wood in the Haute Savoie (Rosemary Ruddle) and in the Pacific Northwest (Shirley Collins). Or it may relate to major

The combination of blue and white is an eternal favorite in kitchens around the world.

pieces of equipment, such as a cloam oven in Devon for making clotted cream (Geraldene Holt) or the butchering table in India (Julie Sahni). Even if it is not manifest on a large scale, the influence of local resources will be apparent in smaller items: the *braxera* for roasting chestnuts in the Basque Country (Mariá José Sevilla-Taylor); the polenta pans and *pignati* of Piemonte (Antonio Carluccio) or the storage cupboard made from packing cases in a pioneer Australian settler's kitchen (Judy White).

In addition, long-forgotten practices have left their traces in the form of furnishings which have become traditional although their origin is forgotten—for example, the *credenze* in Tuscany, which Fulvia Sesani describes in such an illuminating manner. (The same may apply to colors. I was fascinated by Shirley Collins' speculation that the preference of people in Seattle for blue and white in the kitchen may stem back to the china that was the hallmark of the company that established the first Trading Post there.)

How, then, do the size, configuration, and equipment of a kitchen affect its performance? Perhaps the first thing to be said is that there is no necessary connection between large size and good equipment on the one hand and excellent cooking on the other. Gerald Long makes this point quite explicitly, but it also emerges from Rena Salaman's fascinating description of town and island kitchens in Greece, and from the simplicity of the rural Thai kitchen vividly portrayed by Philip Iddison, as well as from several other essays that excellent cooking can be and has been carried out with quite minimal equipment.

This is true of both hemispheres. I was once invited by a Taiwanese couple, in Taiwan, to help prepare a feast. Accepting eagerly, I was taken aback to find myself alongside them in a tiny kitchen equipped with just a two-ring gas burner and a primitive sink. I had to take my cue from the deftness of their own movements and somehow prepare the vegetables without getting in their way. The two gas rings were in use the whole time, and one of them often had a "tower" of steamers on it. The results did indeed constitute a feast.

Yet changes in equipment can be of great consequence, even if they do not significantly affect the quality of the cooking. Several essays, such as those by Professor Smith and Dr Benker, show how significant was the introduction of the stove; an innovation which Gunilla Englund tells us was called "the black sow" in Sweden. Sri Owen explains lucidly why stoves and ranges do not have the same importance in the tropics: but both she and Richard Hosking cite the invention of the Japanese rice steamer as something that has introduced an element of revolution into Asian kitchens in the present century.

Modernization of kitchens might be expected to erode old traditions, especially those which depended on the open hearth. It is certainly true that practices such as smoking foods in the smoke of the hearth fire have necessarily disappeared with the passing of the open hearth. But, to borrow Maria Johnson's telling phrase, the kitchen is apt to be "the most

Eggs for baking are stored at room temperature in a handsome metal holder.

conservative place in the house"—and many kitchen traditions have survived unscathed—sometimes even unnoticed.

Until now I had not been aware that there are religious figures which belong to kitchens and that these can retain a presence in the kitchen however much it is modernized. Now that I have read what Diana Southwood Kennedy, in her vivid essay on Mexican kitchens (including the unforgettable one built around a tree trunk), has to say about the Patron Saint of the Kitchen there, and Clio Whittaker's account of the kitchen god *Zaojung* in China, and Richard Hosking's reference to *Kojin*, the God of Fire in Japan, I am enlightened.

I asked a friend from Laos whether there had been some sort of "god" in our kitchen in Vientiane. Yes, there was a *phi* (spirit) which gave protection to the whole structure, including the kitchen, so long as it was treated with proper attention, which meant taking food from the kitchen to the spirit house every full moon.

My Lao friend also reminded me that a typical dwelling in the Lao countryside would incorporate a kitchen and a living room and a bedroom, plus a bathroom which would be "open," that is to say without a roof; and that this bathroom would be used, logically enough, for washing both people and "the dishes." For this reason the bathroom usually adjoined the kitchen.

Now here is one subject, "washing up," which is not covered in detail by any of the essayists, an omission which is understandable, but which I—a conscientious and skillful washer-up—would like to correct. I have sometimes had fantasies about a future archeologist, seeking to reconstruct domestic life in Britain in what would be for him or her the very distant past, producing a paper with a title like "The Purification of the Dishes in Twentieth Century Britain: Preliminary Findings." He or she would cite evidence from digs in the site of former London to show that the space devoted to washing-up in kitchens seemed to have been greater than that devoted to cooking, and would speculate that for us "ancient Britons" the hallowed pattern of hunting and gathering, preparing the food, cooking, laying the table, and eating (the climax), should be replaced by one which would end with: purification of the dishes (the climax). He or she would then pose the key question: to whom was entrusted this final rite?

Well, although these possibly entertaining fantasies are divorced from reality, the fact remains that washing-up can easily take as long as and require as much effort as cooking. If the kitchen is a theater, as Antonio Carluccio eloquently persuades us, we must not overlook the last scene of each day's performance.

Here I have trespassed from the past into the present, but in good company. If one looks among the essays for accounts of what happens now, one will not look in vain. Essays by Sir Terence Conran, characteristically intent on design, and Gerald Long are among those that provide fascinating glimpses of the present, while showing clearly how the present is built on the past.

Yes, that the past almost always survives in the present is one unsurprising but important conclusion from this collective survey of kitchen history. Despite the present tendency of wealthy people to order a complete new kitchen, the norm has been and remains for kitchens to evolve slowly, and piecemeal. Although Elisabeth Lambert Ortiz's colorful essay must win the prize for taking us furthest back in time—to the Inca kitchens of Peru—it is surely Geraldene Holt's Devon kitchen that best illustrates the theme of gradual evolution, since it incorporates features from the fifteenth century to the present.

There, then, are some of the thoughts that have bubbled up in my mind. Countless others will be provoked by the essays. My real task, which I perform with enthusiasm, is simply to congratulate the authors on providing an international mosaic of kitchen portraits such as, to the best of my knowledge, has never been available before.

Alan Davidson
World's End, Chelsea, London   January 1991

A rugged country interior in which the beautiful centuries-old features are at home alongside more modern conveniences.

ATLANTIC
EUROPE

❖

A Farmhouse Kitchen   Northern France   Amsterdam
A Cottar's Kitchen   Alsace

A Farmhouse Kitchen
In the West Country

❖

GERALDENE HOLT

The tapering peninsula of England known as the West Country stretches from the estuary of the Severn to the Cornish headland of Land's End. Its four counties of Cornwall, Devon, Somerset, and Dorset are renowned for their great natural beauty and mild climate. Although the West Country is predominantly an agricultural area, a fishing industry developed in many of the sheltered inlets of the Atlantic coast, and from the larger ports of Bristol, Plymouth, and Falmouth, West Country seafarers have long traded all over the world, bringing back spices and sugar in exchange for tin ore and china clay.

With the introduction of the coal-fired cast-iron range (above) in the latter half of the nineteenth century, skillful cooks found it easier to control the cooking process. This appliance was the forerunner of the sleek models beloved of interior decorators and cooks today.

The generously proportioned dining table (opposite) was central to convivial feasts attended by family and friends.

For centuries the wealth of the region has been founded on its wool industry from the grazing sheep; its fine cream, butter, and cheese from the dairy cattle; and its cider from the apple orchards. Most of the population lives in villages and hamlets scattered around a local market town—a pattern of living that dates from well before the Norman Conquest in 1066. Many of the fine farmhouses of the area were first recorded in the Domesday Book, the great Norman landholding inventory of twenty years later.

The West Country kitchen that I know best is my own. Parts of our thatched farmhouse date from the fifteenth century and the kitchen, which is remarkably well preserved, lies at the older end. The room measures about 20 feet (6 meters) square and the wide wooden door opens onto the big square farmyard, which is enclosed with barns and byres in the traditional manner of a *barton* or Anglo-Saxon barley farm. Like the other windows at this end of the house, the kitchen window faces away from the prevailing westerly wind.

The flagstone floor of the kitchen remains cool all the year round because the rectangular slabs of smooth shale are laid directly on the soil. The white-painted walls are plastered fairly unevenly over daub and wattle, and the ceiling, which is supported on large oak beams, is also

16

The open-hearth fireplace (top) *in Geraldene Holt's house was once the setting for intense culinary activity, but is now used to house kitchen collectables. Bread was baked in the beehive-shaped wall oven; the hot fuel was raked out before the dough was placed in so that the loaves cooked in a falling heat and gained flavor from the fuels used. After kneading, the dough was left to prove (rise) in a bread crock* (above).

Some cast-iron ranges (opposite, top) *were not only massive but ornate, showing off the industrial skills mastered during the nineteenth century.*

Churning butter (opposite bottom) *was a dull and laborious task before twentieth-century gadgetry took over.*

plastered. On the far wall, well away from the drafts from the door, the wide hearth fireplace dominates the room and takes up most of one wall. Its tall, gently narrowing chimney is built directly above the stone hearth. If you look up the chimney you can make out the mortar lining, encrusted with a thick layer of tar and soot from centuries of wood fires, and a long way above is a small rectangle of blue sky where the chimney finally ends.

Built into the left-hand wall of the fireplace is a beehive-shaped bread oven that probably dates from the late eighteenth century. With family and farmworkers to feed, most of the larger farmhouses in the West Country baked their own bread at least once a week. The oval oven is lined and floored with beautifully shaped blocks of stone, but I have looked in vain for a special "look-and-tell" pebble that was sometimes embedded in the floor of the oven to indicate the temperature by its change in color. An alternative way of judging the temperature was to throw a little flour into the oven to see how quickly it burned.

The bread oven was heated by burning one or two bundles of dry furze, known as faggots. When the flames had died down the ashes were quickly raked from the oven and the bread dough was placed directly on the hot stone floor. The oven opening was closed with lumps of stone, bricks, or a metal door, and the gaps were sealed with soft clay or surplus bread dough. The bread baked in the slowly falling temperature and the finished loaves had a crisp, golden crust, charred in places where they touched the hot stone. As soon as the loaves were baked—they sounded hollow when tapped on the base—they were removed from the oven with a long-handled wooden or metal peel. If the oven was still hot enough, cakes and biscuits, pies and custards would be baked in the residual heat.

A smaller and less common style of West Country oven has been built into the large inglenook fireplace in the sitting room next to the kitchen. This is a cloam oven, named from the Cornish word for clay. Built into the back wall and to one side of the fire, this oven is heated by a flue that conducts hot air and smoke from behind the hearth fire into one side of the oven. Bread could be baked in this oven by placing on its floor a small Roman-style clay oven made by a local potter. This was heated by the current of hot gases passing through, and by surrounding it with hot embers from the wood fire.

The cloam oven was also used for making clotted cream, one of the justly famed foods of the West Country, which is still made in the same way in some Devon farmhouses. An earthenware bowl with sloping sides, filled with cows' milk from the evening milking, was placed in the cloam oven and left overnight for the cream to rise. Next day, using a flat perforated spoon known as a creamer, the thick cream was skimmed from the milk and transferred to a wide, shallow earthenware bowl, which was placed in the cloam oven for up to twenty-four hours. Then the bowl was left in a cool place until the cream had thickened and become clotted or "clouted" with its characteristic granular texture. Clotted cream has the advantage of keeping in a cold larder for up to a week without spoiling.

Until well into the present century, the cook who worked in my kitchen cooked all the food over the large hearth fire. It must have been a tiring and exacting task and not a little dangerous. The fuel, either wood or peat, was burned directly on the stone hearth. In some houses the hearth was paved with bricks or constructed from broken slates set on edge to allow for expansion in the heat. In prosperous households, from the seventeenth century onward, the fuel was burned in a wrought-iron fire basket resting on cast-iron firedogs: the basket contained the fire and helped to concentrate the heat.

Even so, trying to produce a controllable source of heat for cooking must have been frustratingly difficult. Large joints of meat, in Devon most commonly lamb or mutton, were roasted on a spit suspended from a metal bar set into the walls above the fire. Smaller joints were cooked on a movable gridiron fitted with a basting tray.

Substantial stews of boiled meat and vegetables seasoned with garden herbs were the most frequent West Country fare. They were relatively easy to cook and fairly difficult to spoil because an adjustable iron pot crane helped to keep the saucepan in place over the heat. In hard times the meat was replaced by bones alone, and the vegetables and broth were eaten with hunks of bread. In good times home-produced butter and cheese completed the meal—although a thrifty farmer sold all the produce he could at the local market.

The farmer's wife of old took pride in producing as much of her own food as possible. Pigs were traditionally killed in early autumn, so that the ham and bacon would be in good condition for eating at Christmas. Home-cured ham was hung in the chimney-breast for two to four weeks until the smoke from the wood fire had preserved the meat and given it a beautiful flavor.

Simple everyday griddle baking of flat loaves, soda bread, wafers, and pancakes was carried out on a "brander." This was usually a round disk of blackened iron with a hoop-shaped handle over the top, which was suspended from the pot crane or hook.

During the second half of the nineteenth century the coal-fired cast-iron range was developed, and was installed with great enthusiasm in many of the more prosperous kitchens of Britain. The range that once stood in the hearth fireplace in my kitchen was regarded as a mixed blessing by the farmer's wife who cooked here before me. "The wretched thing was a beast to control," she has told me. "It was either smoking and half-cold or, during a gale, the fire burned so fiercely that many's the time that my husband has been greeted by a tray of burnt buns hurled at him when he came home for his tea."

Whatever the disadvantages of the range with its attendant cleaning, stove-blacking, and polishing, its introduction opened up far

Hearth fires were splendid in appearance but difficult to use for cooking, allowing little means of regulating the heat. The most successful recipes were of the long-cooking variety such as stews, while joints were roasted relatively easily on a spit or movable gridiron.

Blue and white china, especially the willow pattern which became popular in the late eighteenth century, is a perennial favorite for displaying on a hutch (dresser). Molds used for making jellies and blancmanges, and jugs of all shapes and sizes, have become the province of the collector.

wider culinary possibilities for the cook—as the recipes of Eliza Acton and Mrs Beeton illustrate. In the right hands the range offered a controllable form of heat with a hot plate, one or two side ovens and even, in some models, a ready supply of hot water that was drawn off from a brass tap near the floor.

All the water for the house and the farm came from the deep well in the corner of the kitchen. Until a few years ago water was raised from the well by a mechanical pump which stood over it. These days we use an electric submersible pump and the soft spring water arrives very cold and with no effort at all.

In the past, as now, the cook's room was the very hub of the house. The fire burned continuously and all the important events of the day were discussed around the large kitchen table that stood in the middle of the room. No doubt there was also a wooden settle with a high back to keep out the drafts and a lidded seat for storage. The family who lived in our house for over a century has told me of the parties and feasts held in the kitchen to celebrate weddings and Christmas, Easter and Michaelmas. Most merry of all were the harvest suppers, when every member of the family and all the farmworkers and friends who had helped bring in the corn, shared a splendid meal of large meat pies and cold ham, served with baked potatoes and freshly baked bread. The apples from the farm's cider orchards had been pressed to make scrumpy and cider, and these powerful beverages were swigged from large china cider mugs. Some West Country kitchens still proudly display these treasures from the harvests of the last century, many of them decorated with verses expressing the honest sentiments and homespun philosophies of the time—some of which seem not inappropriate even today.

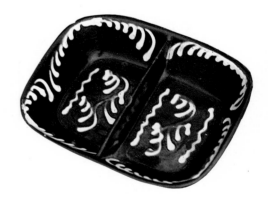

Slipware (pottery decorated by painting with a fluid clay paste) has been made for centuries in many parts of the world. In England, examples of cream and brown slipware abound and were once commonplace in many households. During the seventeenth century, the county of Staffordshire became the main center for its production, the finest examples of which were associated with the name of Thomas Toft. Unlike the simple design shown here, they often featured faces, figures, and ornate curlicues.

Northern France
Town and Country Kitchens

Gerald Long

Calvados (above), a rough brandy made by distilling cider, is stored in a suitably rustic container. Normandy has been renowned for its cider distillation since the sixteenth century. Calvados is categorized according to the number of years it spends ageing in oak casks: "Napoléon," shown here, is aged for over five years.

A Louis XIII-style table (opposite) is set before a wide fireplace used for spit-roasting and grilling.

The development of the kitchen in Paris and the rest of northern France demonstrates that there is no necessary connection between good cooking and good kitchen installations and equipment. For most of the past two hundred years French kitchens, except those of the rich, were poorly installed and badly equipped. Since the Second World War the kitchens have improved greatly; but good French cooking has continued uninterrupted throughout.

The large private houses that were once common in Paris had correspondingly large kitchens, mostly on the ground floor or in a semi-basement at the back of a courtyard with little fresh air or light. Until well into the nineteenth century the most usual cooking range in towns was a box-like construction of fire-bricks, or ordinary bricks lined with fire-clay, with openings in the top of different shapes—square, round, or oblong—set over shafts, at the bottom of which iron grills supported charcoal fires. The ashes fell into a drawer at the bottom of the stove, which also had dampers to raise or lower the heat of the embers. The whole was surmounted by a hood or chimney-breast to carry away the smoke and cooking fumes through either a brick chimney-shaft up to the roof, or a metal chimney set in the wall.

The saucepans and casseroles, of tinned copper in grand kitchens and cast iron and white metal in more humble ones, were either set directly on the burning embers in the openings, or perched on the edge on top. Closed metal containers, or Dutch ovens, placed over the fires were used for baking. Only the largest kitchens had a chimney with an open fire for spit-roasting and grilling. Food was stored in kitchen cupboards, or on shelves, or hanging from hooks, depending on its nature.

Poor homes in towns did not even have a separate space set aside for a kitchen, and at best had only portable containers to hold small charcoal fires, allowing none but the most limited cooking, mostly of soups and stews. Meat was in any case a luxury for the poor.

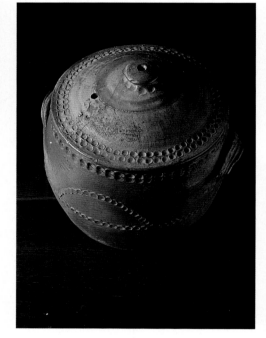

Furniture, ceramics, and copperware from Normandy. Earthenware featured in modest homes, tinned copper in those of the well-to-do. At bottom right, Livarot, a cows' milk cheese from the Calvados region of Normandy, matures for three or four months in a damp cellar. The cheese is nicknamed "colonel" because of the marks left by the five narrow strips of binding originally used to preserve its shape. The brownish red tint comes from annatto, an orange dye.

Cider-making was established in Normandy and Brittany in the twelfth century. Many varieties of apples are used, the majority having a sour taste. Cider is used in fish, rabbit, and tripe recipes.

Bakers sold pastry dough, not always fresh; few kitchens were equipped to make pastries from scratch. Those who could afford them bought grilled meats, small roasts, and stews from cook-shops, which catered for all levels of society. Even today many pork butchers offer a range of cooked dishes.

Sunday roasts, in Paris as in other towns and villages, used to be taken to the baker. This practice has now disappeared, not only because most people have their own ovens, but also because modern bakers' ovens, heated automatically by gas or electricity, heat and cool down rapidly, and have shelves too narrowly spaced for, say, a turkey. The popularity and persistence of spit-roasting, however, is shown by the presence in ironmongers' shops of a small white metal device, the *rôtissoire*. It has a bowl rather like that of a small electric fire, held upright on a stand, with a hand-turned spit through the middle of the bowl. A small pipe at the bottom drains off excess fat. Placed in the hearth, its reflecting bowl turned toward the fire, it can accommodate a chicken, a rolled and boned shoulder of lamb, or a boned joint of *rosbif* prepared in the traditional French manner.

Water for the kitchen came from a tank, replenished daily by a water carrier from a huge barrel on a cart. In 1860 there were 1,253 water carriers in Paris. Piped water gradually became available, but in 1875 half the Parisian houses still did not have it. It was not until 1892 that the municipal office which approved water carriers closed its doors and thus marked the end of a longstanding feature of the social life of Paris kitchens and their cooks.

Piped water came to French villages even later than to Paris and the larger towns, in many cases not until after the Second World War. Before that people drew from springs and wells by bucket or hand-pump. By no means all villages accepted the cost of "town" water when it was first offered: they regarded water as a free supply of nature and wished it to remain so.

In the country only the houses of the well-to-do, those who employed servants, had kitchens in the sense of a room reserved for cooking: they were also the living rooms of the servants. Our house in Normandy is in an area called the Bessin, of which Bayeux is the capital. It was formerly the country residence of a minor nobleman, with part of the ground floor set aside for the farmer and his family. Norman farms had large, wide fireplaces, which were used for spit-roasting, grilling, and stewing in iron cauldrons or earthenware casseroles. The better-off had the same sort of brick cooking stove as in Paris, but fed with hot embers from the fireplace rather than with charcoal. This sort of brick range was called a *potager*, and was often set in a window embrasure just below the sill.

Cooking stoves began to replace fireplaces and the *potagers* by about the middle of the nineteenth century, first as the luxuries of large houses, then gradually filtering down to smaller homes. They were originally fired with brown coal (a fossil fuel halfway between coal and peat) or wood, later with gas. Freestanding stoves of sheet-metal and cast

A charming old-style house in Normandy, a region that rejoices in lavish maritime and agricultural resources.

A large, wide fireplace dominates the kitchen–living room of this farmhouse.

iron came onto the market in large numbers after the First World War, partly because munitions factories found it relatively easy to switch to making them—a version of swords into plough-shares—but they did not become universal until after the Second Word War. Many townsfolk made do with a tabletop cooker of two gas rings; enough, however, to produce the great number of delicious dishes that are the mainstream of cooking in France.

Although gas became available for cooking in the early part of the twentieth century, its acceptance was slow, especially in ovens, in which it was thought to dry out the foods. As late as the 1920s many town kitchens still had coal-fueled stoves. Our village has no gas to this day, and many people depend on bottled gas delivered either in cylinders or by tanker to large permanent reservoirs sited in gardens: we have planted a hedge to hide ours.

Solid-fuel cookers are still very popular in the French countryside. Of modern and practical design, and offering great efficiency in the use of fuel, they heat the kitchen and living room, and often have back-boilers providing constant supplies of hot water. There is still a great deal of wood available for the taking throughout France; it is the usual solid fuel for these versatile cookers in our part of Normandy.

In our neighborhood, as in most parts of France, the local inhabitants tend to leave old houses in favor of recent constructions of cement blocks, the better ones with wooden frames—the standardized products of big building firms. This produces a depressing sameness in the character of towns and even villages. Old houses are often either too big or too small and many need a lot of refurbishing to make them comfortable. They usually come into the hands of outsiders, often from Paris or the local big town, who like "old stones," as the saying goes, and are prepared to spend the money necessary to restore them. Part of the nostalgia of such part-time residents is for low technology, such as wood fires, spit-roasting, and grilling over the embers. Small foundries have dug out their molds for firebacks, while decorated wood-burning stoves and clockwork turnspits are doing a roaring trade.

In the last century our Norman kitchen would have served as the kitchen–living room of the farmer, and probably also his bedroom. It is large, 400 square feet (36 square meters), with a ceiling made from the beams and joists that carry the upper floor. All the beams, and the spaces between, are painted matt white. There is a large former fireplace, but even I have never been tempted to go back to an open fire. We use the chimney for the boilers in the room next door, but have filled in the fireplace opening with glazed tiles. We installed cupboards and working

Freestanding stoves made of sheet-metal and cast iron gradually came into use during the early twentieth century, although many people still retained the open fire as much for its appearance as its functionalism. Coal-fueled stoves were preferred to gas, because the latter was thought to dry out food.

surfaces all round the walls; where there are no cupboards there are steel bars from which copper pans hang on hooks. One door leads into the kitchen lobby and thence to the courtyard on one side and a large larder on the other—cool except in exceptional summers.

We have an open fire in our winter living room. I occasionally, and with some difficulty, roast a chicken in front of it, using a clockwork turnspit and a basket spit (known in France as an "English" spit) in order to keep alive the country traditions and to enjoy the good food that was an inseparable part of them.

AMSTERDAM
A Townhouse Kitchen

ANNEKE AMMERLAAN

The Calvinist way of life was very much in evidence in the traditional Dutch kitchen: both in its appearance and in the type of cooking done within it. In keeping with the religious world-view, which disapproved of anything over-elaborate or highly decorated, the kitchens were functional, clean, and very tidy. The cooking was plain and simple.

The townhouses built in the Concertgebouw area of Amsterdam for the upper middle class at the end of the nineteenth century were typical of these principles. Because land was limited, the streets were narrow and the houses were tall and close together. At the very top of the house were the maids' rooms and underneath these were the family bedrooms. The dining and sitting rooms were on the first floor—called the *beletage* from the French *la belle étage*—and the kitchen was either at street level or in the basement. As it was at the front of the house, deliveries were made to the front door.

The kitchen was a spacious room but often rather dark because of its small windows that did not let in much light, particularly as the narrow streets and tall houses kept out most of the sun. It was simply furnished, and everything was in its proper place. Cleanliness was of the utmost importance, and the building materials themselves were chosen for their ease of cleaning. The floor was covered with black and white tiles of the type that can be seen in the seventeenth-century paintings of Verhoog and Vermeer. The walls were also tiled and the cupboards were usually painted blue, as this was supposed to keep the flies away, although a yellow-beige was sometimes used. The granite *aanrecht*, the work surface, was usually placed along the wall beneath the window, with the sink and water pump at one end in the corner. The chimney that housed the stove was generally built into the opposite wall.

The concern for tidiness meant that everything possible was hidden away in cupboards and drawers. There was a cupboard for staple foods, such as sugar, salt, and flour, as well as for the everyday crockery—the best dinner service was kept in the dining room. This cupboard had glass

Salted and smoked meats and fish are a feature of Dutch cuisine. Whole fish are cooked in a court-bouillon in a long, deep fish kettle. The fish is placed on a removable grid so that it can be lifted from the kettle without breaking. Perforated fish slices (the holes allow the residual court-bouillon to drain away) are used for serving. Opposite: A pristine farmhouse kitchen with utensils neatly in place.

doors through which the shelves could be seen, each lined with a border of checked blue, red or green material. This little shelf border was called a *valletje*, and is still very much a feature of the Dutch kitchen. It also bordered the shelf near the sink where pots and pans were stored. Other pans and utensils were kept beneath the work surface, with cleaning materials under the sink. The cook's knives, such as the bread knife, the meat knife, and the "potato peeler," a very small, curved knife used not just for preparing potatoes but for all vegetables, were kept in a drawer beneath the work surface. The chopping board was wooden, although a material that was easier to clean would have been preferred.

Perishable foods such as cheese were kept in a ventilated cupboard called a *vliegenkast* (fly cupboard); other foods were stored in the cellar, which was usually next door to the kitchen.

If the kitchen was big enough, there would be a large wooden table in the middle of the room. From here the cook ruled her kingdom. The cook was usually an unmarried middle-aged woman, who was in charge of the other servants, also generally female. She was assisted by a young girl, the *keukenmeid*, who did the cleaning as well. There was a big difference between the lives of the servants and those of the family they served. And the kitchen was the servants' domain: the mistress of the house appeared only if there was something wrong; normally, she called the cook upstairs to give her orders.

Many cooks came from Germany or eastern Europe and brought with them their tradition of cake-making and bread-baking. There is no such tradition of home baking in the Netherlands: bread and cakes are bought from the bakers or the patisserie. Applecake was, and still is, practically the only cake made at home: there is a loose-bottomed, round cake tin just for this purpose.

The Dutch are great coffee and tea drinkers and import high-quality cocoa, chocolate, tea, and coffee from Indonesia.

The cooking of Holland owes much to the traditions of Belgian and north German cuisine. The cook, in her well-appointed domain, produces substantial fare. Apart from the European influences, aspects of Indonesian cooking have been adopted by the Dutch. Most notably, rijsttafel—spiced rice with numerous aromatic side dishes—has become a classic.

Food was cooked on top of the stove: even meat, game, and poultry were cooked in a pan over the fire. The wood or coke-burning stove was kept alight all day, because it was always damp in the kitchen, and a large kettle was left permanently on the stove to provide constant hot water for either coffee in the morning or tea in the afternoon.

The atmosphere in the kitchen was made up of different smells. In the morning the scent of the coffee-making mingled with the aromas of simmering meat and vegetables, while in the afternoon you could detect the stock being prepared for the next day's soup and, if you were lucky enough to have a German cook, the smell of freshly baked bread.

The simplicity of Dutch cooking was not only a response to the Calvinist view that food was not supposed to be enjoyed but merely to be eaten in order to stay alive. It was also a result of the abundance of good food available: fish, fresh meat, and plentiful vegetables all tasted very good on their own without elaborate flavorings or sauces.

An ordinary Dutch family started its day with a breakfast of bread, cheese, ham and a boiled egg, and ate their main meal at lunchtime. Only the upper class took dinner in the evening. Lunch consisted of soup, then plain-boiled potatoes and vegetables, with a piece of meat in a simple gravy made from the meat juices, followed by a kind of milk porridge or yogurt. Very often all the courses would be served in a soup plate, which naturally was the most important piece in the dinner service. The evening meal would be simply bread and cheese. In some parts of Holland it is still common for people to have a long lunch hour and to go back home for a hot meal. Because of this, the Dutch have not developed the tradition of entertaining friends over a meal. Instead they invited people after supper and offered first coffee and small cakes, then a *genever*

A small enameled paraffin stove in the much-loved grey and white combination. Below: An array of decorative porcelain molds. Ovenproof porcelain or aluminite is hardwearing and highly suitable for gratin dishes and ramekins as well as molds.

(Dutch gin) or a homemade egg liqueur with chocolates, and later on small snacks.

The plain cooking was also reflected in the utensils of the Dutch kitchen. Only the bare essentials were kept. Like the soup plate on the dining table, the large iron soup pan was the most important piece in the kitchen. At the end of the nineteenth century enameled iron pans were fashionable, and the most popular design was gray with white enamel coating looking like little clouds. As milk was a major part of the daily diet, always accompanying a bread meal, the milk cooker was the second most important pan. This was made of green or gray enameled iron and looked a little like a jug. It had a special lid with holes to prevent the froth of the milk from rising too much. The vegetable colander was also of green or gray enamel and was used to drain the vegetables from the large amount of water in which they were cooked. The frying pan was of thick cast iron with an orange enamel coating. Its color, together with the provocative smell of meat simmering in oil, is a familiar childhood memory for many Dutch people. Meat was cooked slowly in this frying pan either on top of the stove or perhaps on a *petroleumstel*, a miniature paraffin stove. In winter, the frying pan would also be used to make a

stamppot, a meal of potatoes and vegetables cooked together, then mashed with a *potatoemasher*, a typically Dutch utensil hardly ever found outside Holland. Other Dutch specialties were pancakes and *poffertjes* (small yeast-risen pancakes), for which there were also special black cast-iron frying pans: a large flat pan for the pancakes and a smaller one with separate hollows for the *poffertjes*. Molded puddings, such as the *bavarois* for festive occasions, were prepared in white porcelain dishes with matching plates. The most famous of these were made by the Dutch firm Regout, and these and the white dinner service also made by them are now collectors' items.

Any copper pans in the kitchen would be highly polished, since a clean kitchen was the pride of every cook. Enameled tins of sand, soap, and soda kept on the shelf above the sink were the most important products for cleaning kitchen utensils, and were found in every kitchen in Holland, providing almost the only decoration. Although much has changed in the last hundred years, the sand, soap, and soda are still symbols of cleanliness in the Dutch kitchen.

A handsome kitchen with cast-iron appliances and colorful painted furniture. The tradition of furniture painting flourished from the seventeenth to the late nineteenth century and today is enjoying a revival.

A Cottar's Kitchen
A Hebridean Retreat

E L I S A B E T H L U A R D

A *black-house on the island of Lewis in the Outer Hebrides. It was built with double dry-stone walls about 5 feet (1.5 meters) deep. A layer of heathery sods and thatch covered the roof. Inside (above), the furniture was either homemade utilizing timbers washed onto nearby shores, or it was brought back from a trip to the mainland. All items were sturdy and un-adorned. In the main room (opposite), a peat fire burned constantly; smoke escaped through a hole in the roof. The bed at the far end is set into the wall. A line of stones marked the only division between this room and the cattle's quarters.*

For many years as my four children grew up, I was a culinary gypsy of no fixed gastronomic abode. The children have now left home, and I have settled into a Hebridean kitchen on the beautiful island of Mull, home for generations to the distaff side of my husband's family. My Scottish grandmother would have approved.

The two-down, none-up, stone-walled cottage with its 1930s tin-shackery tacked onto the back might seem, to a passing southerner, a typical Highland croft. In reality it is the gardener's cot; the home in the old days of the tied vassal, or cottar, of the "big hoose" hidden in the beech-woods at the bottom of the hill by the seashore. A true croft is the piece of land that supports a crofter and his family, and may not even have a dwelling on it at all.

Occupying the most sheltered spot on the estate, my cottage is perched sentinel on the lip of the 2-acre (1-hectare) stone-walled kitchen garden that once supplied a large Victorian household with all its vegetables and fruit. So far a crop of lettuces, herbs, radishes, and a small neep-and-tattie patch are all I have managed to wrest from the weeds of twenty years' neglect. A pair of moss-draped apple trees, a rhubarb patch, and a few raspberry canes, gooseberry, and currant bushes yield the limited fruits easily grown on these northern islands.

My cottage is, naturally enough, built to exactly the same pattern as a traditional croft dwelling. The black-house that preceded it, and whose stones are incorporated, had curved walls to accommodate the fierce winds from the Atlantic. The chimney-less cooking hearth was at one end of the single room and the family milk-cow provided primitive central heating in her stall by the entrance. The old black-house lacked windows: soot from the fire was far too valuable a fertilizer to be allowed to escape unharvested.

Nowadays we are more modern, with an electricity supply connected not long before I moved in. Until then the house was gas-lit, and the old copper pipes still run behind the wainscot. The kitchen occupies one wall

Elisabeth Luard admits to a love of recycling old furniture. She found the hutch (dresser) that now resides in her kitchen–sitting room in a barn, and set about enlivening it with her own paintings of fruit and vegetables.

Walls and rafters are utilized to maximum advantage as storage space in this traditional country-style kitchen (opposite).

of the sitting–dining room: the living is communal. Most of my larder stores—barley, beans, oats, and flour—are stacked in an old meat-safe, or balanced on narrow open shelves made from a Victorian butler's table. We remain innocent of all but minimal conveniences. There is an electric cooker and a huge elderly fridge that acts as a cold larder, and I admit to a plug-in kettle, but I have no electric toaster. Instead I use a little iron toasting-grid that fits over any heat source and gives the bread a lovely singed flavor.

Pots and pans are tossed into a huge Spanish bread basket under my big wooden table. Made for me by an Andalusian shipwright, the table is far too big for the room, but ever since it arrived in my Spanish kitchen twenty years ago it has been my favorite kitchen tool, my source of inspiration. Its scrubbed boards afford enough space to lay out and admire good raw ingredients—a quarter-bucketful of small speckled brown trout someone has managed to coax out of the burn; crabs and maybe the occasional lobster from the fisherman at Croig; a gigot of year-old wether lamb from the high pastures behind my cottage; wild thyme and fungi—horn-of-plenty, penny buns, oyster mushrooms—from "my" woods; in high summer there are sloes and magnificent wild raspberries, dark as cabuchon rubies, to make into jam. In addition, to spread on the scones that are the daily bread of rural Scotland, the local butcher has hand-churned Islay butter—saffron-yellow, patterned like watered silk and with the slightly soured taste of ripened cream.

On the other side of the table is the old *aig an tein*—the "at-the-fire" room—with an open log fire, augmented with a bit of peat or coal to hold the warmth overnight. The fireplace had been converted in the last century to accommodate a black-iron open range, removed before my time, so the overmantel is high and has a triple flue. Now that this has been replaced with an electric cooker on the far wall, the fireplace is more or less as it was a hundred years ago, with a big mesh-and-brass fireguard round it for drying kitchen cloths, towels, and the wet socks that are the inevitable daily hazard of life on this lush, rainwashed island.

Chrissie MacDonald, my crofting neighbor along the shore who supplies me with orange-yolked eggs from her free-foraging, tufty-topped Hebridean chickens, remembers her unmodernized two-up, two-down cot in her grandmother's time:

> We always lived in the kitchen, there was a sitting room on the other side, but that was kept only for very best—visiting posh folk, a wedding, or for the lying-in before a funeral: you could never have got a coffin up and down the narrow stairs. The sitting room had a carpet on the floor, and we never went in there except to clean, of course.
>
> Our cooking was done in the fireplace within my grandmother's memory: we put in an open range around 1912, and that was replaced with a closed range in 1954–55. My mother still put her hand in the oven to test the heat—she never trusted a thermometer—but then she could put her hand straight into boiling water and lift out a cloutie dumpling [a fruit pudding wrapped in a cloth]. There

Elisabeth Luard spent her early married life in Andalusia where she acquired the large pine table she regards as a source of culinary inspiration. The mermaid lamp was commissioned from the Bloomsbury artist Quentin Bell.

was a black kettle which sat right in the open range and got all black from the fire, and a shiny kettle which sat on the hob ready to fill the teapot.

I remember when I was a child sitting on the kirst—the oatmeal-chest—to turn the butter churn handle. We would sing as we churned, and there was a song-book kept in there: we liked the Irish songs—"Kathleen Mavoreen" and that. My mother used to come in and tell us off for kicking the kirst as we kept time. There were flat basins for setting the milk for the cream to rise, a skimmer to lift it off ready for the butter making. We had a flat rectangular dish, like an ashet but without an edge, with holes in for draining the cream. There were crocks for the milk—tall, made of glazed earthenware. There was a mold for the butter with a thistle on it for best. For everyday, the butter was always patted with a criss-cross pattern before it was put on the table. There was beestie cheese, the first of the year, after the calving: that was so rich and thick, mother cut it off in slices to lay it on the scones. All the dairy implements had to be scalded and set to dry, never washed with soap.

There was no need to keep cake in our house, as there was always baking. We had the girdle for scones and oatcakes, with a hinged handle over the top for hanging over the fire, and we had a pair of irons for drying the oatcakes. The boiling pan was the three-toed pot, which stood by the fire or could be suspended above it. There was a pail of water behind the door for cooking. Water for washing and for washing-up was put in the middle of the table after the meal. Fetching the water from the well just outside was the children's job, and we really hated it: it was cold and damp and heavy. Now we have the same water piped in, but Father still likes his straight from the well.

I, too, pipe my water down from the spring up the hill, but there are times in high summer when the supply is down to a trickle and we have to use the bath as a reservoir. And there are times too in the winter when the pipes freeze, and I have to fetch a bucket from the running stream at the back to cook slow one-pot stews that require minimum liquid and very little washing-up.

Limitations on conveniences intensify experiences. Spring is not simply a matter of sunshine and blossom, when there are new beech leaves and hawthorn buds to be gathered for a salad. The appearance of the first shoots of wild garlic among the bluebells is greeted with genuine delight. Nettle-tops and bracken shoots add fresh flavor and vitamins to a barley-thickened stew. By mid-July the first chanterelles appear in the woods—easily gathered, and infinitely more delicious than any cultivated mushrooms. And it takes less time to throw up a batch of scones, or put a loaf of bread to rise, than it does to drive to the nearest shop.

Limitations on space, too, create their own pleasures. Preparing meals at one end of the communal living room places the cook firmly at the center of the household, not tucked away behind doors peeling potatoes. There's no doubt it's cramped, particularly when there are grown-up children or visitors sharing the living space. It's rather like living on a boat—everything has to be stowed away in its proper place as soon as it's used, so there can never be piles of washing-up in the sink.

I like the arrangement. It allows me a certain theatricality in my presentation of the food I have prepared. Conversations can be interrupted to draw attention to a girdle-full of scones, a pile of steaming crabs, a particularly fine apple pie: it all builds up anticipation for the meal ahead. Delicious scents from the cooking pot add an edge to appetites already sharpened by the display on the table: a hot-pot of home-grown potatoes layered with wild mushrooms, a silvery salmon so fresh there is a creamy curd between the rosy flakes of flesh. Was ever a town kitchen, with its access to all the world's store-cupboard, so blessed?

A blazing fire and a collection of tartan rugs add visual and physical warmth to this rugged interior. Tartan is part of the heritage of the Scottish Highlanders, with each clan boasting a design unique to itself. Before the advent of commercial dyes, Scottish women made the dyes from vegetables native to the Highlands.

ALSACE
A Country Household

❖

MARIE-NOËLE DENIS

Breitenback in Alsace (above). This eastern province of France is noted for its rich, hearty fare—a mix of French, German, and Jewish influences—and its distinctive white wines. Fruits such as cherries, plums, pears, and apricots are used in tarts and to make the exquisite eaux-de-vie (unsweetened fruit brandies) (opposite). Among the best known are Kirsch, which uses fermented cherries, and Poire William, which is made from pears, one of which—tantalizingly—is preserved inside the bottle. The aromatic flowers of fruit bushes such as elder are prepared as fritters.

In common with all traditional homes in the nineteenth century, the kitchen in Alsace had a clearly defined position in the overall plan of the country household, a position closely linked to its practical and symbolic functions at the heart of the home and family, and which existed until the end of the Second World War.

The kitchen was usually situated at the back of the house. It looked out onto the narrow alley between it and the next building, and was reached through a door from the entrance hall. It lay between the living room, or *Stub*, looking onto the street, and the scullery, where vegetables were kept, looking onto the yard. In well-to-do households a second living room, the *Kleinstub*, sometimes came between kitchen and scullery.

The kitchen was first and foremost the "water room" of the house. Its floor was therefore covered with sandstone flags or tiles, while all the other rooms in the house had wooden floors. Water for cooking was brought in buckets from the well in the yard. The buckets were stored on a low rack near a sandstone sink under the window, which drained into the alley. There was often a second sink in the scullery, and this was used for the dirtiest jobs.

The kitchen was, however, also the "fire room." The only chimney in the house was set against the partition wall that separated the kitchen and the *Stub*. Although the house was timber framed, this particular wall was of stone to guard against fire. All the fireplaces in the house were here, under a vast hood that collected smoke and steam: the grate of the heating stove in the *Stub* was reached, and therefore stoked, from the kitchen; there was a great brick cooking stove, and another for cooking animal feed. At right angles was the entrance to the bread oven, the main part of which was on the outside of the house to avoid excessive heat and the danger of fire when the bread was baked each Saturday.

This monumental construction has evolved over hundreds of years. At the end of the Middle Ages people were still heating their food over open fires, on a brick platform under a hood. Until quite recently this hood

opened directly into the loft. This and the smoke-blackened beams can still be seen in southern Alsace, where the ancient building methods have survived. In the seventeenth century the chimney-flue was extended up to the roof and a cupboard installed in the loft through which the smoke could be diverted. This was used to smoke the family bacon.

Apart from these basic fixtures, there was little other furniture in the kitchen. (On the whole, only the more public rooms were furnished.) Kitchen furniture was always pine, and very plain. It was found in the kitchens of only the most prosperous families. As late as the nineteenth century, only 13 percent of the tables and 4 percent of the chairs in an average household were situated in the kitchen. Women worked standing up, with only the sink or the cooker to lean on. Buckets were put down on three-legged stools, and a chest of firewood might serve as a seat.

Closed cupboards were rare. Nineteenth-century household inventories indicate that only one family in four owned a kitchen cupboard. This was usually a roughly built pine dresser divided into two sections: a closed lower section with one or two doors and, above it, a series of shelves with beading along them to prevent objects tipping over. On the shelves were displayed flower-painted earthenware plates given as wedding presents, and some pewterware.

The great stoneware storage jars (for lard or vinegar) sat on the floor. Hand-held utensils made of iron or copper, such as skimmers, ladles, and cooking spoons hung over the cooker, under the hood. Saucepans and their lids were stored on a wooden rack or bar attached to the cornice. Other shelves lined the walls and housed containers made of iron, cast iron, copper, or glazed pottery. These included saucepans, frying pans, stewpots, earthenware dishes, and various kinds of cake molds, each for a different occasion: *Kougelhopf* for the Sunday brioche, crayfish for wedding cakes, a baby for christenings, a fish for New Year, a star for Christmas, and a *fleur de lys* for Epiphany.

A kitchen with multiple hearths (opposite). The brick-built cook stove, the access to the grate of the Stub heating stove, and the oven for preparing animal feed are lined up under a vast hood. Glazed earthenware crockery is arranged on the shelves of the pine hutch (dresser).

Originally, the Baeckeoffe (right) was cooked by the village baker and prepared by the housewife the previous night. Monday—washing day—was usually the appointed day for this ritual, as the women were too busy with their chores to cook. Their husbands took the casserole of marinated meat and vegetables to the baker on their way to the fields to work. The name of the dish comes from baeken (to bake) and Ofen (oven).

Cheeses produced in Alsace (far right) include Laguiole, a relative of Cantal. Its slightly Cheddar taste is well suited to cheese tarts, of which there are countless versions nationwide. The most famous Alsatian cheese is Munster. It has the dubious honor of being one of the smelliest of all cheeses, but has its enthusiasts. It is made in small, flat rounds (shown here), has a smooth, soft consistency, and is often served sprinkled with caraway seeds.

The kitchen was used only for the preparation of food. Even in the most humble households, people never ate there as they did in other parts of France. Masters and servants took their meals together in the *Stub*.

The arrangement of the kitchen fireplaces meant that foods that were boiled or stewed in flat-bottomed, lidded earthenware vessels and oven-baked cakes were more common than foods grilled in frying pans or cooked in metal casseroles. Daily fare consisted of vegetable soup and pork, potato soup, simmered slowly, thickened with fresh cream and served with sausages, sorrel soup, pea soup, or lentil soup, cooked in water with bacon.

On Sundays the mistress of the house cooked *pot-au-feu*, a stew of boiled beef and vegetables; sauerkraut with pork; *Baeckeoffe*, an oven-baked hotpot of beef and pork, marinated in white wine and stewed with potatoes and onions in an earthenware dish. She also baked a *Kougelhopf* (sweet yeast bread with dried fruit and almonds) and fruit tarts. On Saturdays she baked the week's bread, a *tarte flambée* of onions and bacon, and *Flammekuche*, which was made with a portion of the bread dough.

A special cake was baked to celebrate each religious or family festival: *Männele*, little men made of brioche dough for St Nicholas (December 6th); *petits fours* made with butter, aniseed, or cinnamon for Advent; Christmas cake decorated with a little baby or a star; Twelfth Night cake; fritters for carnival time; lamb-shaped biscuits for Easter.

Women also had the care of the lowly animals that were essential to feed the family. They prepared food for pigs and poultry in the kitchen or scullery and cooked it in the stove kept specially for this purpose. Grandmother, being less active, was in charge of the fires. She kept a particular eye on the stoking of the *Stub* heating stove, and made sure that the lanterns, oil lamps, and candlesticks left on the cooking stove during the day were extinguished.

As the hub of their activities, the kitchen was a vital meeting place for women, their refuge from isolation at the heart of the family. Here, while standing at their work, they would receive fleeting visits from neighboring women who came to borrow spices, a recipe, or a misplaced kitchen utensil.

Changes in lifestyle have profoundly affected this traditional kitchen and, in its latest incarnation, the kitchen is tending to take the place of the *Stub* as a dining room, and even as a living room. This change has come about through a reduction in the size of the family group, with fewer children and no servants; through the modernization of heating methods, the use of wood-burning cooking stoves made of enameled cast iron, and of modern gas or electric cookers; and through the introduction of piped water. The kitchen now contains a dining table, a bench, and chairs arranged in a corner just as they used to be in the *Stub*. Kitchen utensils are hidden away in "rustic Louis XV-style" fitted cupboards and the litter of cushions and knick-knacks appears to deny any culinary use. The modern Alsatian kitchen looks like a sitting room.

Numerous doughs and pastries are essential to the cook's repertoire for a variety of cakes, biscuits, and breads. These include the Christolle, a fruity yeast cake served at Christmas, for which the dough is rolled out and folded one half over the other to suggest the swaddling clothes of a newborn baby.

CENTRAL
& EASTERN
EUROPE

❖

*Bulgaria   Russia   The Swedish Kitchen
Bavaria   The Alpine Cook*

BULGARIA
Changing Rural Kitchens

M ARIA J OHNSON

Until the beginning of this century, the room that housed the fireplace in the town and village homes on the northern flanks of the Balkan mountains was known either as prust, *hall, probably because it was the largest room in the house, or* kushti, *literally "the house", because it was the most important part of the dwelling. The Bulgarian kitchen acquired its present-day name,* kouhnya, *comparatively recently.*

This wool carpet (above) is not woven, but consists of tightly pressed layers of unspun wool. The technique has been lost and one can only guess how it was made.

A nineteenth-century kitchen (opposite). Bulgarian hand-woven rugs are characterized by bright colors and bold patterning.

A few years ago, I had an opportunity to see a number of authentically preserved nineteenth-century Bulgarian kitchens in the high village of Bozhentsi (now a museum), which is pleasantly situated near the town of Gabrovo in the Balkan Mountains.

The houses were all built between the end of the eighteenth and the turn of the twentieth century. Each had either three or five rooms on a single level, with extensive cellars where the wine and sauerkraut barrels must have been stored, and an attic where choice bunches of grapes from the family's vineyard were hung from the beams. An external wooden staircase led to a wide covered verandah, and the first and largest room of the house, the cook's room. This room contained the fireplace and was the most conservative place in the house in both composition and meaning: the elements in the room and their arrangement had been the same for centuries, and it had always stood as a symbol for domestic life. The room had a carved ceiling, and its scrubbed wooden floor was covered with colorful hand-woven rugs.

Despite its considerable size, the cook's room was lit by only one window, which had wooden shutters and was located in the back wall. At night, the custom was to secure the shutters from the inside, and place a candle on the sill of a small, window-like opening in the dividing wall between the cook's room and the *soba* (guest room-cum-bedroom) to illuminate both rooms. The light from the candle and the flames from the fireplace were the only sources of light in the cook's room.

Built like a stage proscenium, the wooden bonnet surmounting the fireplace in this kitchen in central Bulgaria lends the room a curiously theatrical air. The settee is made of wood. The house itself was built around 1853. Long domination by the Turks has left its mark on the cuisine of Bulgaria, as the long-handled pot in the hearth illustrates.

In the houses of Bozhentsi I could see no cooking stoves or ovens, so the dough for the bread must have been kneaded and shaped in the cook's room, then baked in the ashes of the fire, or carried, probably on boards, to the village bakehouse. The open fireplace was positioned—in the Balkan tradition of the last few hundred years—in one corner of the cook's room, between the back outside wall of the house and the wall shared with the *soba*, which had a brick heating stove, backing onto and heated from the fireplace in the kitchen. The two sources of heat were connected by an opening in the wall.

The semicircular fireplace was imposing: at least 3 meters (10 feet) wide, its interior was roughly built of brick or stone. A flue went straight up the chimney, which was covered with a small roof. Most of the fireplaces in the village had flat open hearths made of beaten clay.

Over the fireplace was a semicircular carved wooden bonnet, suspended from the ceiling, known as *kemer*. The walls on either side were covered with built-in cupboards, their doors carved with geometrical motifs. Among these cupboards were a number of paneled niches, all housing various pots and pans, condiments, and fireplace equipment.

The most important pieces of kitchenware (and obligatory items of a bride's dowry) were a number of tinned copper vessels: *sahani*, deep plates with graduated lids; *tendzheri*, large stewpans also with graduated lids; *tigani*, large frying pans; and *tepsiya*, the largest and shallowest Bulgarian pan (up to 1 meter or 40 inches in diameter) in which meat was roasted and pastry baked. In addition, there were many earthenware plates, cups, casseroles, and bowls glazed in warm earthy colors, plus assorted cutlery.

A beautiful feature of the cook's room was the long storage shelf, *politsa*, around all four walls, about 30 centimeters (1 foot) from the wooden ceiling, on which gleamed an array of small copper vessels, glazed clay plates and pots, and other household objects that were not needed for everyday use.

Vrushnik—a metal pan with a lid for baking bread in an open fire or charcoal oven. The vrushnik had to be buried under the burning wood, resulting in a uniquely flavored bread.

*Skillful embroidery, frequently in reds and black, is
worked on linen using silk or wool thread. This
room adjacent to the kitchen holds wooden utensils
for storing cheese, flour, and other staples.*

Folk art painting (top left) on furniture and other utilitarian objects flourished throughout Europe from the late sixteenth to the early twentieth century. The trend for ornamentation often found its way onto the facades of buildings, and both secular and religious images were depicted. This house in Koprivshtitza in central Bulgaria was painted by Kosta Zograph. A siniya (top center), a low copper table at which the family took their meals, sitting or kneeling on the pillows on the floor. The kitchen sink is on the left, with the vodnik adjacent to it. Traditional individual pots (top right) in which food is cooked and served, and a glazed stomna for water. A long storage shelf (above left) extends right around the room and houses platters and copperware. Food (above *center) is set out on the sofra, a low wooden table. Pastirma, dried beef coated with spices such as paprika and chili pepper, is served thinly sliced with bread, or fried in butter and eaten with fried eggs. Stews of meat and vegetables are seasoned with spices and topped with yogurt and eggs. Pies, tarts, and festive breads (above right) come in numerous varieties.*

In the absence of an indoor supply, water was carried from wells and courtyard fountains in a host of vessels. The shapes of these utensils reflect the cultural influences of Russia, Greece, and Turkey, Bulgaria's neighbors. The copper pans are also called siniya, like the low table.

There was no running water in the nineteenth-century Bulgarian house, so all the water for drinking, cooking, and washing had to be brought from the village fountain, or from a well sunk in the courtyard. This task was usually performed by the young girls in the family who carried the water in tinned copper cauldrons, *kotli*, slung from a yoke over one shoulder, or in unglazed earthenware pitchers, *stomni*. In the cook's room, the water was kept in a special place, *vodnik*, near the entrance door. The *vodnik* consisted of several large wooden hooks, on which all the water-filled vessels were suspended.

Time has stood still in the houses of Bozhentsi, and the kitchens that once bustled with life and laughter now lie dormant as museum pieces. In his novel Zhenitba ("Wedding"), nineteenth-century Bulgarian ethnographer and novelist Tsani Ginchev described what people cooked in similar kitchens in the nearby town of Lyaskovets:

> *Preparations started a week before the engagement feast. The eldest son, Dobri, and his youngest brother went to the nearby village of Kozarevsti and bought a fatted pig for roasting. Then four turkeys, three geese, twelve hens and a ram were slaughtered and cooked . . . Black pepper was ground, hot paprika pepper was crushed, rock salt was pounded and sieved . . . Early in the morning of the engagement day four batches of white bread raised with a sourdough starter were baked and wrapped in hand-woven towels. The pig was killed; washed with hot ash water and cleaned.*

In those days, everyday cooking was normally carried out by the women of the household—the mother and her unmarried daughters or daughters-in-law. However, the roasting of meat for special occasions was the responsibility of the head of the family or another man known in the community for his knowledge in these matters. For the engagement feast described by Ginchev, the roasting of the pig was entrusted to Grandpa Minko, who was recognized as the expert in roasting whole animals.

His first task was to order his helpers, a couple of younger men, to preheat the oven in the *peshtnik* (oven room). This was a separate building in the courtyard that was used as a summer kitchen. A wood fire was laid on the floor of the oven and when an acceptably high white heat was reached, the burning embers were scraped out and the floor of the oven wiped clean with a wet rag mop fastened to a long handle.

Grandpa Minko knew exactly when the oven was ready to take the pig: his "thermometer" was a handful of tow (short pieces of flax or hemp). When it was thrown into the oven and blackened without a blaze of sparks, he knew that the oven was ready for roasting. In went the pig, stretched on its belly in a huge, tinned copper pan over a bed of twigs. The air-vent at the top of the oven was closed and luted round with clay, and the oven mouth was stopped up with a thick stone slab and sealed. This done, the pig was left to roast for about five hours in the gradually diminishing heat, until cooked to a turn. And cooked to perfection it must have been, as anyone who has had the good fortune to taste meat roasted in such an oven will attest. I have feasted on suckling pig cooked in a similar village oven and the meat, seasoned with the clean mountain air, was the most delicious food I have ever eaten.

A winemaker displays the roast sheep he is about to serve his guests. Bulgaria produces both red and white wines, and is noted for its slivovitz, a colorless spirit distilled from plums.

The outdoor oven room was traditionally used as a summer kitchen.

RUSSIA
Cooking in a Peasant Hut

❖

R. E. F. SMITH

The traditional Russian peasant dwelling of round timbers was a feature of the Slav colonization of the vast forests of the European plain. Such huts had originated before the Mongol invasions of the thirteenth century, and remained characteristic of the European colonization that continued even into the seventeenth century. The crucial feature of such a dwelling was that it was heated, as is indicated by its Russian name—isba. This term, in fact, has a common root with the English word, stove, which itself formerly indicated a heated room. Often, these dwellings consisted of only one room, so the cook's room was also the room for all the family and, given the severe Russian climate, sometimes its livestock as well.

The earliest stoves seem to have been little more than a hearth of clay on a layer of broken and pounded pots with a more or less circular wall enclosing the fire. But from the twelfth century a new kind of stove appeared. It was probably of similar form, sometimes enclosed by a dome, but now the fire or oven was built on a raised clay-covered timber platform supported by, usually four, timber feet driven into the ground. A small pit was sunk into the floor under the stove, probably as a dry storage area. The height of the platform varied: in the nineteenth century it was determined by the height of the woman of the house, but a sixteenth-century illustration shows the cook having to stoop to reach it comfortably.

Cooking with these domed stoves was unpleasant in other ways, too. When the fire was lit, smoke poured out of the mouth of the stove and left a thick layer of soot in the room; this process was accurately called "heating blackly." Yet the stoves survived in some remote and, presumably, impoverished areas, where as late as the 1880s they were still being built. Cooking methods were rather limited. Bread, pasties, and pies could be baked directly in the ashes or on the floor of the stove immediately after the fire had died down. Most cooking pots were deep, bowl-like shapes, suitable for the other main foods in the Russian diet: porridges, soups, and stews. These were

The sturdy, monolithic ovens that dominated the cook's room in the wealthier households (above and opposite) made way for a more sophisticated range of cooking techniques than those afforded by the domed, smoky stoves common in peasant dwellings. There was ample space on the surrounds of the more "modern" ovens to store pots, irons, butter molds, and other equipment.

usually based on vegetables, with occasional additions of fat, meat, or river fish, often preserved in brine, and could be left to cook overnight or while working outside. Shallow earthenware dishes—rather like sauté dishes or frying pans—were also used. These were all flat bottomed since they sat on the floor of the stove.

From the sixteenth century, first smoke pipes (unlike chimneys in that they were not directly connected to the stove, and which often had fretted decorations), then true chimneys began to appear. These must have made conditions somewhat more comfortable for the cook, but otherwise made little difference to the cooking processes. However, at about the same time a major change was gradually taking place in the stove itself.

In the dwellings of rich townsfolk, flat-topped stoves, massive structures now often regarded as the traditional Russian stove, were becoming increasingly popular. The introduction of these stoves, derived from Western models, increased the risk of fire in rooms fitted only with smoke pipes; this encouraged the spread of true chimneys directly connecting the stove to the outside of the house. This gave a greater draft, but also allowed the cook to control it more effectively. A different risk arose from the much increased weight of the stove, which could no longer be supported by the relatively light platforms on which earlier stoves had been built. In 1718 legislation in Moscow attempted to insist that stoves be "built on the ground, not on a framework."

Erratically and over a long period this new kind of stove was adopted by the peasantry, and by the late nineteenth century it was widespread. It remained in use into the 1930s, when there were some 20 million of them in Russia. This stove made considerable changes to life inside the peasant's hut: it provided more warmth; people could sleep on top of it or on shelving nearby; and in some parts of the country the stove was even used as a steam bath. Cubby-holes in the massive walls were useful for drying wet clothes. In addition to the residual heat of the oven itself, these spaces could be used to dry fungi gathered from the forests and foods to be stored for the long winters. The dry space below the platform was used for storage.

Preparing food in a modern Russian kitchen. The stove remains a source of warmth through the long cold winters.

Stores of this kind often took up as much as a quarter of the area of the room. The space between the mouth of the stove and the opposite wall was the cooking area. There was a small movable table, but the rest of the items were fixed: a bench, sometimes incorporating a small cupboard, the top of which served as a work surface; and a cupboard about 5 feet (1.5 meters) high with four or five shelves. The latter sometimes concealed the entry to the cellar, essential to store food for the long winters. The beam separating the cooking area from the rest of the room was called the pasty beam; this was where bread and other dough-based food was kept. Here, too, an easily tilted water container was suspended on a rope or chain with a tub beneath. Sometimes a curtain reinforced this boundary. When facing the stove, the

A local fruit and vegetable market. Sweetened red fruits are used to make kisel. *The fruit is cooked to a purée thickened with arrowroot or flour, and occasionally flavored with white wine. The dessert is served warm or cold. Strawberries, rhubarb, cranberries, and tart red apples are commonly used in this dish.*

cook was on the left side. This was not merely a development based on convenience for right-handed cooks, it was also a feature noted from Mongolia to Ireland: that women had the left and men the right side of the family hearth.

Apart from the stove, there were few other changes until the late nineteenth century. Cooking equipment included containers for bread, salt, grain, water, and honey, as well as tubs, bowls, and a trough in which to make dough. All these were of wood, either solid wood or the thick bark of birch or lime. The sourdough for the rye bread was prepared in a wooden trough in the evening and left to rise overnight. It was placed in the oven with a long-handled wooden shovel with a fine, broad edge. Wooden gingerbread molds have been dated back to the eighteenth century. Sweetstuffs were made by smearing the abundant forest berries with honey on a wooden board and setting it to dry either in the sun, or by the stove. This process was repeated until a thickish, pastille-like sweet had been formed. Drink was served by wooden scoops; food was eaten mainly from wooden bowls by means of wooden spoons.

Earthenware cooking pots show little change in shape over long periods of time. A poker to place the logs in the stove and plates for baking pasties were used in advanced areas toward the end of the nineteenth century. These, together with knives and choppers, were probably the only metal items used in the traditional kitchen.

The cooking area in the Russian peasant house, even at the beginning of the twentieth century, included many primitive elements. However, from the late nineteenth century industrialization has made an impact on this relict culture. In 1917 two-thirds of the Russian population were peasants; today less than one-tenth live in the countryside and, of those, peasants in the old sense are a small proportion. The traditional Russian rural culture is largely vanishing.

THE SWEDISH KITCHEN
A Century of Change

❖

GUNILLA ENGLUND

Because of its thinness and crispy texture, knackebrod is as much a biscuit as a bread. It is made mainly from rye flour; until the mid-nineteenth century rye was the staple grain for breadmaking in northern Europe, grown for its ability to tolerate colder conditions than wheat. Only in recent years have the texture and flavor of rye flour been appreciated in Western households, where wheat flour has been considered superior for decades.

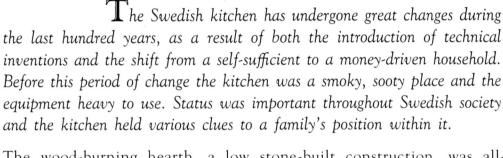

The Swedish kitchen has undergone great changes during the last hundred years, as a result of both the introduction of technical inventions and the shift from a self-sufficient to a money-driven household. Before this period of change the kitchen was a smoky, sooty place and the equipment heavy to use. Status was important throughout Swedish society and the kitchen held various clues to a family's position within it.

The wood-burning hearth, a low stone-built construction, was all-important. It fulfilled three functions: as a cooker, as a source of warmth, and as a source of light. The fire in this hearth was never allowed to die out, and it was considered an embarrassment to have to go to a neighbor for a light. The family gathered round the hearth in the evenings and worked in the glow from the fire. In winter, to save fuel, the kitchen was often the only room in the house that was used: the family not only ate in it but also lived and slept there.

A three-legged iron pot was the most widely used container for cooking—primarily for boiling. If a family owned copper pots, which were much more expensive, they were displayed prominently in the kitchen as a sign of wealth. The roasting spit and gridiron were also important pieces of cooking equipment. The Swedish verb *steka*, meaning "to fry," comes from a verb signifying the roasting over a fire of spiked meat or fish. Spit-roasting, however, was high-quality cooking in the nineteenth century and certainly not something that peasant households could readily afford.

Daily food was monotonous, though for a special feast everyone prepared as much of a spread as possible. It was usual, then, particularly among the peasants, for a family to bring its own food to the feast, which could last for several days. The Swedish peasants rarely ate fresh food; it was said that they preferred preserved food, a fact commented on by several centuries of foreign travelers to Sweden. Their food could be salted, dried, smoked, or pickled. Drying and smoking were the earliest

As in other Scandinavian countries, Christmas festivities commence on December 13th, St Lucia's Day, with the main Christmas meal served on Christmas Eve. Caramelized ham with apples, red cabbage and mustard are traditional fare. A julhog is frequently a feature of the Christmas table, often consisting of a "tower" comprising a round of rye bread, a wheat bun sprinkled with large sugar crystals, a heart-shaped loaf or piece of shortbread, and a red apple.

A wood-burning hearth with a bread oven set into the wall beside it (overleaf). Apart from cooking, the kitchen was also the focus of weaving and sewing.

methods of preserving food. Salt, on the other hand, mostly had to be imported, for Sweden produced very little of its own. Its importance in food preservation meant that as far back as the Middle Ages, the Hanseatic League (a confederacy established in 1239) had wielded great power as controllers of the supply of salt.

During the days of self-sufficiency, it was imperative to store away enough food during the autumn to last the family throughout the following year. Crops were harvested; pigs, sheep, and goats slaughtered. Cows were seldom slaughtered—only when they had become too old to yield milk—and horses were rarely killed for their meat, even during times of hardship, for it was seen as a great humiliation to have to eat horse meat. Horse slaughterers were firmly at the bottom of the social scale (many also worked as executioners).

A family's status was elevated by having a well-stocked larder. It was usual among the peasantry, for example, to bake bread (*halkaka*) twice a year, though bread for feast-days was baked separately. It was a sign of poverty to have to bake several times a year: a poor family had to buy flour whenever it had the means, rather than in bulk a couple of times a year. The bread became progressively harder and more sour the older it got. *Knackebrod*, a wafer-thin crispbread made of rye and corn, was baked with a hole in the middle so that it could be strung up for storage.

66

Bread was baked in an oven set into the wall of the hearth, either above the fire or beside it. In some parts of the country there were special public baking ovens where women baked together, and they often helped each other with certain other tasks, such as cheese-making. Then they would meet at a chosen house, each with her share of the necessary ingredients. The finished product was shared among them.

The principle of the self-sufficient household was that the whole family would contribute to the provision of nourishment for its survival. Women carried out every job connected with the care of the household. As well as the cooking and household chores, they made most of the clothes and domestic textiles, although it was not until the nineteenth century that curtains at the windows and rugs for the floors became widely used in rural homes. Men worked the farm. They also generally made the kitchen equipment. Most of the utensils were fashioned from wood, including massive mixing bowls, chopping boards, storage containers, whisks, and ladles.

Thrift was an important quality in a housewife and naturally the woman's skill in running the home was a precondition of the family's survival. Even if it could afford not to, the family always lived thriftily on workdays. The equitable distribution of food among the members of the family was also important, even though the man's and woman's portions were not equal: it was always assumed that men needed a larger share than women.

Before rugs became a feature in homes during the nineteenth century, women tarred their timber floors to preserve them (above). Baking bread in a traditional kitchen (below).

During the nineteenth century this pattern shifted appreciably, as industrialization brought with it the rise of an urban middle class. In these new middle-class circles, a man was expected to be able to provide for the whole family. Thus the wife was not expected to work: if she did, the husband's status was reduced.

The introduction of the iron stove in the mid-nineteenth century also brought great change, though initially it was greeted with considerable scepticism. It was nicknamed the "black sow" and people doubted whether it could really be used as a cooker; nor did they believe in its ability to provide heat, and worse still, it definitely did not give out light. Charles Emil Hagdahl (a cookbook writer known for his book *The Art of Cooking*) maintained that meat cooked traditionally on the spit was much juicier, thus retaining its essential nutrients, whereas the meat juices in a pan on the stove collected at the bottom of the meat, leaving the upper part dry and unpalatable.

The appearance of the paraffin lamp in the 1870s was a decisive factor in the eventual success of the iron stove. Once paraffin was used for lighting, and the stove or hearth fire was no longer the only source of light, it became easier to use several rooms in each dwelling instead of just the kitchen. For those households with a Dutch-tile stove, heating was no problem either.

Gas and electric cookers were not introduced until the beginning of the twentieth century and met with similar resistance: many cooks felt that foods, whether cooked on top or inside the cooker, were simply not as good. The gas cooker was also considered to be dangerous—a large number of people believed that the gas could penetrate their food.

The refrigerator was an invention of great significance. In 1925 two Swedish engineers, Baltzar von Platen and Carl Munters, succeeded in building a refrigerator that worked on the absorption principle. The invention aroused a lot of interest both in Sweden and abroad. At last a reliable way of preserving fresh food had been developed, for the precursor of the refrigerator—the ice chest—was nowhere near as effective, and it dripped, too, as the ice melted. Electrolux set up a factory in 1925 and, though initially expensive, by the 1930s the refrigerator had become a common sight in people's homes.

The tradition of using wood to fashion kitchen utensils such as spoons and chopping boards (top) has been upheld despite the move towards "easy-care" plastic and metal. Wood's only drawback is that it must be scrubbed to keep it scrupulously clean; it has no place in the dishwasher as it can warp and split. Floral china (above) is another hardy perennial with an appeal that never wanes.

The modern Swedish kitchen was also born in the 1930s. It was purely functional. This was the age of the built-in kitchen—cookers, sinks with drainers, refrigerators, and cupboards—the type of equipment that only the Swedes have made a longstanding custom of leaving behind for the new owners when they move house. The materials (aluminum, tin, enamel, stainless steel, and plastic) and the variety of new electrical gadgets significantly reduced the effort needed in the kitchen. The 1930s kitchen was a small room, for it was assumed that housewives would not spend much of their time cooking now that canned and processed foods were available in the shops. It was a radical idea that few could aspire to, particularly as a great many Swedes were living under straitened circumstances during that period.

Clean, uncluttered lines and the use of white offset by colorful accessories are classic elements in Swedish design (opposite).

BAVARIA
Kitchen and Cuisine

G E R T R U D   B E N K E R

Smooth timber and rough-textured stone—building materials for centuries past—make a modern alliance in a kitchen–dining room that draws its warmth as much from its mellow color scheme as its open fire. Rugged features are offset by the sleek, pristine black cooktop and its New Age wok.

In the past—and particularly in the days of open cooking fires—the Bavarian kitchen was a dark and sooty room, whether it was in an urban home or a farmhouse. Urban kitchens responded to change much faster than those in the countryside, and it was well into the twentieth century before kitchens in rural areas were brightened up to bring them a little closer in style to the urban ideal of a shining, labor-saving laboratory for food preparation. Perversely, these town kitchens are now undergoing another change, reflecting people's desire for a kitchen that is not just functional but also comfortable. Thus highly practical and hygienic designs and synthetic materials are on the way out as people try to recreate "grandmother's kitchen" and to preserve the traditional ways.

In Bavaria (as in the whole of southern Germany) the kitchen—that is the room containing the stove and facilities for the preparation of meals—has developed differently from the "hall-house" of lower Saxony. As far back as the late Middle Ages, the Bavarian kitchen was separated from the living room. The kitchen had an open fire for cooking, but people ate and relaxed in the other room. Depending on the size of the farm and the number of people to be fed, the farmhouse kitchen was either a dark corner of the entrance hall or a large workroom close to the living room. From this position, the living room's tiled stove could be used (usually from the rear). Soot and smoke remained the hallmarks of these cooking areas until the mid-twentieth century and many women suffered eye disease as a result of the poisonous smoke fumes.

For centuries, the open wood-burning stove with a hood to deflect sparks and/or a flue above it was the familiar cooking fire. Because of the risk of fire, fireplaces, even in wooden houses, were mostly arched constructions of stone. Firewood was stored in a space beneath the stove so that it could dry out. The stove itself was usually made of quarry tiles or

An open wood-burning stove with arched base. The blackened wall serves as a reminder that the fuel would have rendered the kitchen smoky and uncomfortable.

brick and was approximately 3 feet (90 centimeters) high with a surface area of 3 to 6 square feet (1–2 square meters).

Around 1800, fuel-saving closed stoves with suspended cooking pots began to appear in town houses, but this development did not reach country areas for another sixty to 100 years. The economy stoves, which were usually made of cast iron, included devices for baking and roasting, and were often linked to the living room stove. One type peculiar to east Bavaria was the oven positioned against the living room wall. Pipes made of iron or earthenware penetrated deep into the furnace area, and peels (long poles with prongs at the end) were used to push in the cooking pots. This kind of oven engendered its own particular style of cooking—one-pot meals, soups, and potatoes in their jackets.

In many parts of Bavaria electric cookers were not introduced until after the Second World War. Electric lighting was installed in towns from 1900 onward, but, again, did not reach the countryside for another fifty years. In addition to the light given off by the glowing cooking fire, people used pinewood tapers fixed in various holders and stands, and tallow or oil lamps set in niches on the wall or attached to the ceiling.

In the days when the open fire flamed or glimmered on the hearth, pots made of clay or iron were set beside the fire or on tripods over it. Pans of various sizes were suspended over the heat by means of a crane with hooks and chains, or on tripods. In these was cooked a porridge or purée made either from milk and grains or from water and pulses. Deep pans were for festive baking, when wheat flour doughnuts and cakes were fried in hot fat. Soups were made in large kettles suspended over the stove area and were eaten daily. In east Bavaria, a special boiler built into the wall of the living room stove was used to heat liquids.

Crockery, pots, and pans were stored on shelves and tiered storage racks. Until the nineteenth century, the only cupboards in the kitchen were small, single-door larders known as *Almer* or *Bhalter* in which were stored foodstuffs such as milk, bread, spices, cheese, and tea. During the nineteenth century, a new item of furniture, the hutch or dresser, appeared in town kitchens, and reached the farmhouse kitchens early in the twentieth century. It consisted of a base cupboard with double doors and a glass-doored upper cupboard for crockery. This kitchen cupboard is still used in some small farm kitchens, although prosperous modern farmers progressed long ago to the high-tech, built-in kitchens of the Frankfurt type first introduced in the 1920s.

Walk in pantries were used for storing provisions. They contained storage racks for milk-skimming equipment, barrels for cabbage, and bottles and pots for every kind of vegetable. Sometimes a cellar, reached down a few steps from the kitchen, served as a food storage area.

Storage cupboards gradually evolved from sturdy plank constructions to relatively sophisticated hutches (dressers) complete with glass-doored tops.

An outdoor oven (top) copes with large batches of tasty bread.

Many kinds of bread are made (above), including wholewheat and rye varieties flavored with sesame or cumin. The special flavor of rye bread comes from the sourdough starter; in its simplest form this is just an old piece of bread dough from a previous batch, moistened with water. Starters are also made from fermented flour, water, and sugar.

The wood-burning stove (opposite) has been the traditional Bavarian cooking fire for centuries. This is a relatively recent model; the earliest were simply open hearths.

The introduction of refrigeration brought about a fundamental change in cooking methods, even in farmhouse kitchens. The refrigerator made it possible, and simple, to preserve meat and fish as well as home-grown fruit and vegetables.

In the past, massive chopping blocks and low rectangular tables served as work surfaces. On these meat was chopped, game plucked, fish scaled, and vegetables prepared: a universal piece of furniture for all kinds of food preparation. Nowadays it is very rare to find such a piece in use: they have been replaced by built-in work surfaces and tables. In any case the need for such a surface area has considerably diminished now that even farmers' wives buy semi-prepared or ready-cooked foods.

However, the long-established culture of Bavaria and its strong ties with the land provide a rich heritage with which to counter the effects of the introduction of foreign dishes and the uniformity of modern cooking. The reappraisal of traditional dishes is seen as a means of preserving the friendly and hospitable Bavarian way of life.

Because the "land" of Bavaria encompasses some very different terrains, it is difficult to generalize about a "Bavarian cuisine." The great variety of dietary and cooking tradition is largely due to the geology and climatic conditions of the various areas.

The fertile loams of the pre-Alps, the Isar valley and the Rott valley, and the wind-deposited loams of the Gäuboden areas beside the Danube, are excellent for growing cereal crops. Rich flour-based dishes and dumplings developed here, while the sterile sandy soils and inclement climates of the mountainous areas in the east—the Bavarian Forest, Oberpfalz, and Oberfranken—produced a more meager diet. Until well into the twentieth century, daily fare in these regions consisted simply of soups bolstered with potato dishes. The frugal inhabitants of this area accepted the potato very early—its cultivation began before 1700. In contrast, potatoes—even in the form of dumplings—were only hesitantly accepted in the fertile regions of south Bavaria.

The lush meadows and pastures of the rainy pre-Alp region, particularly in the Allgäu, are perfect for grazing animals, and the area became known for its milk and cheeses. Dishes combining flour and cheese (such as cheese noodles, *Käsespätzle*, and south German ravioli, *Maultaschen*) are still very popular there. In central and lower Frankonia, the sandy, loamy soils and mild climate favor viticulture and fruit growing, as well as the cultivation of vegetables.

While everyday dishes have always been determined by local produce, the nature of festive meals is firmly based on tradition and beliefs. Festive meals are more copious and richer than daily fare. In some areas, meat was normally eaten only on Sundays, but there was a sumptuous array of roast and baked dishes for the high church festivals such as Christmas, Easter, Whitsun, and church consecrations. The well-known caricature of the portly Bavarian munching his leg of pork and raising his beer tankard does not give a true picture: he is really found only on special occasions.

THE ALPINE COOK
And Her Kitchen

❖

ROSEMARY RUDDLE

Decorative detailing (top and opposite) is minimal in the wooden houses of the Haute Savoie, with protection from the elements being the prime concern. The region is noted for a variety of fine cheeses (above). The buttery Bagnes is much favored for raclettes, while Cantal, Tomme de Savoie, and the softer Reblochon also play a significant part in the cook's repertoire.

"**I** *can tell when to put more wood on the stove,*" *says my friend in her Alpine kitchen in the Haute Savoie region of France.* "*The cooking pots go quiet and when there's no sound of simmering soup, I know I must open the stove and put in more logs.*" *Logs are something she has plenty of. When she opens her carved wooden shutters, with their design of hearts, each morning before breakfast, she sees from her kitchen window the wooded slopes, pines and larches predominating, that are the source, not just of her fuel, but also of the building material for all the local houses. The woods belong to the Commune, but inhabitants can apply for a permit to clear and keep the fallen trees left by avalanches. Outside each house is a large neat stack of logs to last through the winter.*

In the Haute Savoie, the mountainous region bordering Switzerland and Italy, winters are traditionally long and hard. In the past, once the snows came, the valleys were cut off from the outside world. The cook had to be resourceful enough to ensure that the family was self-sufficient, and at the same time had to make the cheese and butter that would support them through the winter months. In a climate like this, nothing could be left to chance, and those who lived in the Haute Savoie learned to be independent, self-reliant, and above all, practical.

A neat design solution to the two problems of cold and hunger evolved. The wooden houses were built on two levels: cows, hens, and the pig (usually fattened and killed for Christmas) were kept in a barn underneath the living quarters of the family. The wooden floors between the two allowed the warmth from the animals to act as a primitive central heating system; moreover, supplies of fresh milk and eggs could be reached simply by climbing down a ladder, an important consideration when a heavy fall of snow could make it impossible or at least extremely difficult to leave the house.

Wood was the basic material from which the Alpine house and most of its contents were made. It was also the means of survival. The focus of the kitchen–living room was the sturdy wood-burning stove that steadily devoured the piles of timber gathered from the nearby slopes. It was wood that cooked the food, heated the iron, and made tolerable the sleeping quarters in the chilly rafters. Also housed in the rafters were the salted and smoked hams that were suspended there from hooks to mature.

The kitchen, incorporating the dining and living space, centered on the wood-burning stove, and its chimney-pipe warmed the sleeping quarters situated on a platform in the rafters above. (The roof was insulated with hay which was simply removed in the spring.) The bedrooms were small and simply furnished: there was little decoration and no rugs on the wooden floors. Everything possible was done to keep out the cold. The windows in all the rooms were small and never on the north side. Old bedcovers were often used to make thick curtains—indeed, anything warm was utilized.

A "vaulted" kitchen hutch (dresser) built to fit a curved recess. This and similar constructions served as storage space for essential dry ingredients such as flour, rice, and polenta. Like the general design of the house, these handsome cupboards were unadorned save for the simplest carving. The quality and texture of the wood were considered sufficient decoration.

Almost everything was made of wood, including the walls, the floor, and the roof. A simple wooden table was used for preparing and eating food. Wooden chests held the winter's supply of flour, rice, polenta, and *crozets*. There were carved wooden spoons, a wooden box to keep salt in, and wooden shelves for storing the cooking pots (made of tin, iron, or copper), the *caquelon* or fondue pot, the plates and dishes. Jugs and bowls were made of wood, too, using a local method of working pine and larchwood together. The *seille* was a jug made in this way, which was used for milking and carrying water.

For fondues, quiches, and the grilled sandwich known as croque-monsieur, Comté (also called Comté Gruyère) is the ideal cheese. It varies from ivory to pale yellow and features the characteristic small holes that one associates with Gruyère-type cheeses. Comté's flavor is less sweet than that of its Swiss counterpart. The rind may be gold or brown. The first dairy to make Comté was recorded in the thirteenth century. Manufacture is governed by an appellation d'origine, the name Comté being followed by details of the department or district in which the cheese was made.

The use of rice and polenta reflects the proximity of the Italian border. (Haute Savoie, now part of France, was an independent duchy until the nineteenth century.) *Crozets* are a local specialty made from potatoes and flour. A grayish sand color, these tiny squares are prepared during the summer and dried for use in the winter, when they are cooked in boiling bouillon for ten to fifteen minutes, drained and served *au gratin* with cream and cheese. Batches of densely textured *pain de compagne* were once baked by each family in communal village ovens, lit for one day to make all the bread to last the winter. In some remote valleys villagers made a loaf capable of being kept for up to six months.

The kitchen shelves also stored *eau de vie*, flavored with the juniper berries that grow all over the slopes, and jars of honey with flavors so distinctive that the cook could tell if the bees were collecting pollen on the higher slopes covered with Alpine flowers, or from the pine trees, or from the chestnuts lower down the valley. *Fraises du bois*, bilberries, and raspberries grow wild and were picked in season to fill fruit tarts and, more importantly, to make into jams and jellies, also stored on the wooden shelves for wintertime, when they might be eaten with fresh *fromage blanc* and cream as a treat.

The soup simmering on my friend's stove is probably the same recipe as the one her grandmother made with root vegetables—carrots, cabbage, and potatoes, which can be kept throughout the winter—for *le souper* or evening meal. Sitting round the table by the stove, the oil lamps lit and the shutters closed against the cold, the family waited for the cook to ladle the broth and vegetables onto a large slice of toast in each soup plate. Traditionally, the evening meal was a simple one, often consisting only of fresh creamy milk in a two-handled bowl, bread, and cheese.

The main meal was at midday. Game from the woods might be available to the cook, although hunting was strictly controlled. (During the Second World War the rules were relaxed because the population was starving, resulting in the near-extinction of many local species.) More often there were homemade sausages of pork and cabbage eaten with potatoes, a piece of pot-roast pork interlarded with cheese followed by the *farçon* or *farcement*, two variations of a dish made with potatoes and prunes. All were substantial meals to keep out the cold.

The resourceful Alpine cook has found many delicious ways of combining the basic ingredients of cheese, white wine, bacon or raw ham, and eggs. These dishes do not take long to prepare—the cook is too busy with milking and making butter and cheese, such as Gruyère, Comté, Cantal, and the various Tommes de Savoie. The most prized are those made in the summer, when the cows graze on the Alpine grass enriched with flowers, then matured to eat in winter. At their best they are eaten simply with bread.

Other dishes were invented to use up the ends of the cheeses and stale bread, and, some would say, to put to best use the rather acid local white wine. Two of the most renowned are *croûte savoyarde*, a large slice of country bread covered with slices of cheese, moistened with white wine,

and baked; and *fondue savoyarde*, for which a mixture of local cheeses is melted with white wine and a dash of *eau de vie* in a *caquelon*, into which pieces of bread, speared on long-handled forks are dipped.

When summer came, the cows were taken up to the high pastures to graze, as indeed they still are. The cook's center of operation moved too. The summer chalets are simple wooden structures, buried in snow all winter. They usually consist of one room with a hay-loft above. The large coppers for cheese-making take up most of the space, and an open hearth is used for cooking and for warmth at night. It was at this hearth that a piece of dry cheese, the end of a large cheese, would be speared on a stick of larchwood and toasted in front of the fire. This is the origin of the now-famous *raclette*. As the surface of the cheese bubbled, the cook took a flat, spatula-like wooden implement and scraped off the runny cheese. A large wooden bowl of potatoes in their skins went with the cheese, and, perhaps, some pickled onions or gherkins. To make a richer meal the family might carve slices off a ham, which had been smoked in the chimney and hung from hooks in the rafters, or off a piece of cured beef called *grisons*. A *raclette*, say the locals, never tastes as good if it isn't made like this, for all the convenience of new implements designed to hold the cheese under a special electric grill.

Cantal is thought to be the oldest of all French cheeses and was mentioned by Pliny the Elder nearly 2,000 years ago. It is matured for three to six months, developing from a smooth-textured, nutty-flavored cheese into a crumbly, sharper-tasting commodity. It has a dark brown or gray rind streaked with red; the cheese is ivory-colored. Cantal is used in numerous regional dishes such as aligot, a mixture of potatoes, garlic, milk, and melted cheese. The basic methods of farmhouse production have remained unaltered for centuries.

MEDITERRANEAN & SOUTHERN EUROPE

❖

*La Foncubierta   Provence   Piemonte   Pasus
The Tuscan Kitchen   Two Greek Kitchens*

LA FONCUBIERTA
A Cortijo Kitchen

ALICIA RIOS

A *patchwork of olive groves* (top); *the facade of
La Foncubierta* (above); *and one of the kitchens of the
Palacio de Viana in Cordoba city* (opposite).

La Foncubierta is a cortijo or farming estate in Andalusia,
the region of Spain that spreads right across the south of the Iberian peninsula, forming the southern border of Europe.

Andalusia is a seductive land, with undulating hills covered in olive groves gently dipping into valleys of cereals and sunflowers. It is one of the oldest regions in the Mediterranean, with historical links to many ancient cultures. Under the Romans, Andalusia was the most civilized and heavily populated of the senatorial provinces. It was pre-eminently an agricultural region dominated by large estates (*latifundio*) with three basic products—wheat, wine, and oil. With the Moorish invasion, it became the most Islamic of the Spanish regions, but remained largely agricultural. Hispanic then Moslem trade routes flourished and declined, but in their place new paths were marked out by those heading for the New World, and the profitable exchange of goods continued in Seville.

Today the area outside the large towns of Andalusia consists of villages inhabited largely by casual farmhands, with a small percentage of craftsmen still engaged in activities closely linked to the *latifundio* agricultural system.

The concept of the *cortijo* goes back to the Roman *latifundio*, which developed into Moslem settlements called *alcarias*. The present *cortijos* were built in the seventeenth and more particularly the eighteenth centuries, preserving the baroque character of the *alcarias*, but incorporating more mundane features as well, such as whitewashed walls, glazed earthenware bricks, and strong railings.

A typical *cortijo* consists of a large patio closed off at the front with a wall in which a gate bears the family shield. Inside are various buildings: the main house belonging to the owner of the estate, the tenant farmer's and manager's houses, and sometimes more modest accommodation for seasonal workers, plus all the structures necessary for the working of the farm: stables, wine cellars, granaries, and the oil mills or *almazaras*.

Until about 1925 some seventy people lived at La Foncubierta. There were about fifty yokes of oxen, pigs, and two oil mills. The olive pickers also lived on the farm from November to February, which meant housing another 160 people. At its height the *cortijo* maintained four houses in full operation. The only house still perfectly maintained is the main house, inhabited by the present owners, Señor Cristóbal Lovera Prieto and his wife María Pilar. The estate is about 20 miles (32 kilometers) from Cordoba, near La Rambla, a village famous for its pale earthenware pottery, from which is made the pitchers that have been used throughout Spain for centuries.

The kitchen of the *cortijo* is its social core and is always a hive of activity. It is a kingdom of power and wisdom in which the cook rules over her territory, respecting and reinterpreting the rules of her art, which have been passed down through the generations. The whole kitchen exudes grace and love. Light streams in through the windows during the day and at night the modern electric lights are backed up by olive oil lamps and candles for emergency use in power cuts. The colors, sounds, and aromas are constantly changing, reflecting the time of day, the season, the number of people to be fed, and the wealth of traditional celebrations that are the heritage of this part of the country. The cook makes the most of all the treasures available to her: the orange and olive groves, the vineyards, the almond trees, and the livestock. There is also plenty of game, and both freshwater and saltwater fish.

The curvilinear and geometric design of the mosaic floor dominates one of the patios of La Foncubierta.

In La Foncubierta there are really three kitchens: the owner's modern kitchen, the slaughter kitchen, and the country kitchen. The country kitchen is the smallest of the three, and is sometimes called the kitchen of the first communions and christenings, as it is next to the large entertaining rooms and gives onto a charming patio with a fountain and leafy trees.

About thirty pigs are killed every winter at the *cortijo*, and four butchers and four women come from the village to help with the slaughter. In the slaughter kitchen, hams and chines of pork are cured and various kinds of sausage are made: the spicy *chorizo* sausage, blood sausage, and fried bacon sausage. There is a large hooded fireplace and a wooden beam from which containers hang. The hearth is at floor level and pots are suspended over it. Inside the chimney is a grill made of wood and iron with hooks on which to hang, smoke, and dry the sausages and hams.

Reflecting the forces of nature, there are four clearly defined elements in the *cortijo* kitchen: fire, water, air, and earth.

Fire has been constant throughout the mixed cultural tradition of Andalusia. Roman ovens were fueled with olive branches and charcoal, and the Christian kitchen featured a hearth for stewpots and casseroles. The Arabic customs required a fire for frying in large deep pans.

The hearth is lit early in the morning to brew coffee and fry bread for breakfast, then the pot is put on the stove to prepare the daily stew. In

Spanish ceramics (top) were much influenced by developments in Byzantium and the Islamic world. These plates and vessels are rich in color and bold in their design and execution, contrasting markedly with the unadorned jugs (above) whose appeal lies in their seductive shape.

The modern kitchen at La Foncubierta (above left) is a happy mix of traditional elements and labor-saving devices.

the Andalusian farmhouse kitchen just about anything goes into the pot, which is covered and left to cook slowly throughout the morning. Meanwhile a *sofrito*—a highly flavored seasoning made by crushing garlic, pine kernels and cumin, then adding tomato and a generous dash of oil and vinegar—sizzles away in the frying pan. Nowadays there is a modern cooker fueled by butane gas under a traditional extractor hood, fitted into a green marble slab. The back wall is protected from the heat by some beautiful traditional Seville tiles. The same tiles are used to border the whole room.

Water is very much part of the life and culture of the region, necessary for the high standards of cleanliness demanded by the impeccable Andalusian women. There are deep marble sinks in the kitchens, and a well and fountain outside.

Air is an essential element in the *cortijo* kitchen: it dries the sausages and circulates through the *fresqueras*, the ventilated cupboards where food can be stored without refrigeration. In the pantry, cool air is essential to keep food fresh and stop the oil from turning rancid.

The floor of the *cortijo* kitchen is made of baked earth, the walls of lime, the pots and mortar of earthenware. The walls and storage shelves of the pantry are all made of earth, as is the traditional oven in the country kitchen.

The kitchen usually has two large work tables. One is made of wood, with a rush-bottomed bench beside it, painted red or green. The other is a marble-topped table used especially for making cakes and fried doughs. There are also work surfaces around the wall. An important feature is the high stool, which is ideal for sitting on while pounding ingredients in the mortar, or as a support for the *dornillo*, the earthenware bowl used for making summer *gazpachos*.

The cupboards are true treasure chests. They are made of wood and lined with starched, embroidered cloths. They have wickerwork doors, with shelves for storing the pots and pans, crockery and spices, and sometimes hooks to hang up cups or utensils. A handy cupboard near the stove contains garlic, salt, oil, vinegar, cumin, cinnamon, orange and lemon peel, pine kernels, pepper, paprika, and oregano, as well as wine for cooking, the pestle and mortar, chopping boards, knives, and the sharpener. There is a small drawer for the bottle-opener, corks, string, candles, matches, and other odds and ends.

There is usually a great variety of receptacles, including aluminum saucepans, a few iron or enamel pans, earthenware pots and dishes, a steamer, different sized frying pans, both deep and shallow, and a selection of paella pans. There are griddles for grilling fish and chops, and maybe an electric fryer. There is sometimes a pressure cooker, but microwave ovens are rare as they do not suit traditional Andalusian cookery. The main utensils are various sizes of spatulas and draining spoons for fried foods and tongs for the grill. Other kitchen utensils include the grater, mincer, and colander, and of course a variety of knives, large spoons, and ladles. Of great importance are the containers for clean

A vast cupboard, the alacena con vajilla, *houses fine china at the Palacio de Viana in Cordoba city.*

Beautiful and valuable copper cooking pots, a feature of the traditional cocina Cordobesa.

oil and oil that has been used for frying. The used oils are kept separate in labeled containers made of aluminum or stainless steel.

The pantry is a room in its own right with white tiles from floor to ceiling. Hams and sausages hang from hooks on the ceiling, while non-perishable staple foods are stored on shelves: garlic, dried sweet and hot peppers, onions, potatoes, rice, pasta, sugar, oil, wine, local cheeses, dairy products, and the things for the children's *merienda* or teatime.

The day's meals change with the seasons to make full use of local ingredients. Breakfast consists of milky coffee or thick hot chocolate, toast with oil and salt or butter, or maybe fried bread with sugar and cinnamon. In winter it may include eggs, Serrano ham, or garlic soup.

In winter, the first course at lunch is often a heavy soup containing beans, lentils, or chickpeas. Main courses include Andalusian *cocido* or stew, clams in matelote (tomato, onion, and garlic) sauce, roast pigeon, chicken fricassee, kidneys with rice, ham stew, pigs' trotters in batter, meat and potato stew, fried fish, cannelloni, and paellas. *Migas*, a local dish of fried breadcrumbs, is provided for the workers. In summer there are *picadillos* (finely chopped peppers, onions, tomato, and cucumber), *gazpachos*, salads, and other cold dishes using eggs, fish, or larded meats. Typical desserts are fruit compotes, quince jelly with cheese, fresh fruit, fried doughs sweetened with aniseed and honey, and pastries based on fruit and almonds.

Contemporary Andalusian cuisine combines a lively mixture of traditional home cooking and modern ideas to provide meals which may be more practical and less time-consuming to prepare, but are certainly no less tasty or nutritious. The *cortijo* kichen, too, encompasses modern appliances within its beautiful walls, while preserving all the grace and splendor of its origins.

A sturdy mortar and pestle.

PROVENCE
A Designer's Kitchen

SIR TERENCE CONRAN

Vines span the fields at the foot of mountains (above).

Provence yields a diverse range of produce (opposite).

We live in that wonderful region of Provence where small mountain ranges looking as if they have been sculpted by Henry Moore sprout out of green valleys that produce the finest vegetables, fruit, olive oil, purple garlic, and the freshest wine in the whole of France. This sheer abundance of local products, combined with the intense aromatic flavors of the herbs that cover the rocky hillsides, and scent the air and the food, have been the inspiration behind the design of both our kitchen and our cooking in Provence.

Our home in Provence is a nineteenth-century farmhouse built to a formula originally proposed by a Tuscan Count and reproduced many thousands of times across northern Italy and southern France. The typical arrangement is to have two barns with the farmer's living quarters sandwiched between. When we converted the farmhouse a few years ago, one of these barns became our kitchen, laundry, and larder.

In designing our Provençal kitchen, I used the same basic principles that I have used in countless other kitchens over the years. The cooking and preparation area was visually segregated from the eating area, so that the cook could work unimpeded by friends and relations but could join in the conversation. I created a cool shelved pantry in which raw materials could be stored, and designed open shelves on which the pans and kitchen utensils could be kept readily to hand, rather than hidden away in cupboards. The work surfaces were clean, uncluttered, and well lit. I felt that it was important to keep "labor-saving" electronic gadgets to an absolute minimum, and to use natural ventilation to keep the kitchen cool by allowing a draft of air to pass freely through the room.

The particular qualities of our Provençal kitchen are its size, a wonderful beamed ceiling, two enormous french windows opening onto the farmyard and chestnut avenue, with green fields and herb-covered hills in the distance, and its smooth cool stone floor.

Because we live in the house mainly in the summer, it was important to make the kitchen as simple and spacious as possible. We installed a huge refrigerator with an ice-making attachment and disguised its bulk by setting it into the wall. We have two ovens and cooktops, one electric and one bottled gas, and a working top grill with its own built-in extraction system. This is supplemented by an outdoor grill built rather like a pizza oven, which is often used when we want to cook over wood or charcoal.

The wall behind the dining table is "decorated" with everyday cups and plates set on narrow shelving (above). An oak work table defines the limits of the food preparation area (right).

The beautiful Chaîne des Alpilles in the west of Provence rivals the scenery in the verdant valleys and along the glittering Mediterranean coastline.

The plan of the kitchen is very simple. Down one wall runs a continuous work surface made of solid oak. Into this is set the cooking equipment and a pair of glazed stoneware sinks. Simple white-painted cupboards run beneath, filled with cleaning materials, kitchen linens, and those pieces of kitchen equipment that are used only occasionally and which we probably don't really need.

Above the work surface is a broad oak shelf that takes all the pans and casseroles in daily use. Under the shelf is a continuous strip of tungsten lights shielded from the eye by an oak baffle. This space between the shelf and the worktop is covered with cream beveled-edge tiles that were originally designed for the Paris Metro. They are practical to clean and reflect the light from above onto the work surface.

One small but useful detail: the two draining boards fixed to the workbench are angled so that water from washed pots or wet vegetables drains into the sinks rather than forming pools on the work surface.

The opposite wall of the kitchen is entirely covered with shelving, with a long, cool, cantilevered white marble shelf at waist height. Behind this is a continuous strip of mirror about 18 inches (45 centimeters) high and slightly angled to reflect the contents of the bowls and platters of vegetables and fruit that are so prolific and beautiful in this region of France. This display is really the main feature of the kitchen and immediately grabs your attention when you enter the room. It would be appetizing enough without being doubled in dimension by the mirror, but with it you are immediately reminded of the splendid profusion of produce found in the local markets.

Above the display of fruit and vegetables are narrow shelves right up to the ceiling, which hold the plates, dishes, bowls, and mugs in daily use. They bulge out in the center to provide semicircular shelves that comfortably hold large china soup tureens and vegetable dishes. There is so much beautiful china, earthenware, and porcelain, much of it from the region, some of it old and precious, some of it cheap and everyday, so why hide it away in cupboards?

Beneath the marble counter is a long slatted shelf that holds bowls of the less colorful and photogenic vegetables, like potatoes and onions, and storage space for large heavy casseroles that are hard to lift down from high shelves.

The single most important thing in the kitchen is the huge freestanding oak work table which both visually and physically divides the work area from the eating and more decorative area. It's about 3 feet 6 inches (1 meter) deep, 5 feet (1.5 meters) long and just over 3 feet (90 centimeters) high, with two drawers for gadgets and cutlery, and a knife rack at one end. It was made at our workshop at Barton Court from very rough planks of oak, the sort usually used for gateposts, full of knots and character. The top is 3 inches (7.5 centimeters) thick and the fissures and knot holes are filled with black resin.

The work table is large enough for three people to work around: chopping, peeling, podding, slicing, and filleting without getting in each

other's way. The knives are to hand and the wooden spoons and spatulas are kept in a pot. The olive oil from our own trees is stored in a glass bottle, the shape of the Eiffel Tower, and the sea salt in an earthenware bowl to keep it dry. There is usually a pot of basil and a jug of parsley on the worktop.

The other table is also in oak but of a rather finer nature. It is 10 feet (3 meters) long and was made in our workshops by Ed Nicholson. It's a really fine example of English craftsmanship and can seat at least twelve people, fourteen at a pinch. Narrow benches run the length of the table: I enjoy sitting on these extraordinary examples of French utility furniture, circa 1945, which have great style and comfort.

So this is the simple workshop in which many a marvelous Provençal meal is prepared and eaten. Its walls and ceiling are painted a pale bluish grey, the two crossbeams of the rafters left in natural timber with the adze marks still clearly visible. A band of blue, which the flies are supposed to detest, separates the ceiling from the walls. It all adds up, I believe, to the perfect kitchen for a hot climate. Any further embellishment would be superfluous because the wonderful colors and textures of the fruit and vegetables and the shapes of the kitchen utensils, bowls, and dishes are the best decoration you could hope for.

Dishes termed à la provençale *often feature olive oil, tomatoes, and garlic. Ratatouille (above) is one of the best-known vegetable dishes. It originated in Nice, and versions of it appear throughout the region. Zucchini, eggplant, sweet peppers, and tomatoes are often included.*

PIEMONTE
A Center of Hospitality

❖

ANTONIO CARLUCCIO

This house in the Aosta valley (top) is festooned with corn left out to dry. Coarse-ground cornmeal (above) is used to make golden polenta.

A painted room of great charm (opposite). Its walls are hung with wooden and copper utensils.

I come from Piemonte, the northwestern corner of Italy, where I had the advantage of growing up in two very different areas. For my first ten years I lived at Castelnuovo Belbo in the province of Alessandria, where the land has broadened out into fertile plains; after that my family moved to Ivrea in the Canavese, at the head of the Aosta valley in the foothills of the Alps.

Throughout the Italian countryside, the kitchen is the most important place in the household. For Italians, eating well is an enormously enjoyable activity. The kitchen is a social place where everybody meets at least twice a day and where vigorous and sometimes passionate family discussions take place.

In the theater of the kitchen, the housewife is planner, producer, and director. Eventually she will receive an accolade, but only if she has satisfied everyone. Naturally, to achieve this, to provide the good food that acts as a catalyst in keeping families together with warmth and love, a great deal of attention is needed. Unfortunately nowadays the television, which seems to be on all day, including lunch and dinner time, has a prominent place in many kitchens. Those who no longer take advantage of their mealtimes for lively conversation and an exchange of gossip miss out on much of the quality of family life.

The day-to-day running of the kitchen takes time and thought. Creativity and organization are needed to plan meals properly so that the same menu is not repeated too often; wisdom, too, is required to make the most economical use of the freshly bought ingredients from the market. The cook's aim is to titillate the palates of all the diners (*commensali*) with dishes that reflect the cook's skill and talent according to the particular occasion.

In Piemonte it is important to draw a distinction between more affluent people and those who live a simpler life, and also between city dwellers and those who live in small villages. In all cases the kitchen is

A bottle of grappa and a long-handled cooking vessel used in making polenta. Grappa is a spirit, the Italian equivalent of the French marc, *which is savored for its strong, assertive flavor. It is distilled from the mass of pulp, seeds, and stalks that remain after grapes have been pressed for making wine. Particularly in the northern provinces, it is not only drunk but used in recipes such as guinea fowl in red wine,* sciatt (*small cheese fritters*), *and* fave dei morti (*dead men's beans*)—*biscuits traditionally eaten in many parts of Italy on November 2nd, All Souls' Day.*

important. However, those with money to spare will be inclined to have a kitchen designed by a more-or-less famous designer, which may be in plastic or stained wood or even in marble with all possible modern appliances, but no microwave—even in these days, when the speed of life makes dedication to the preparation of food more difficult, the microwave oven is absolutely taboo. Statistically it has been shown that Italians possess the smallest number of such appliances in their kitchens and also keep the fewest products in deep-freezers.

These designer kitchens tend to have lost the natural warm atmosphere of a traditional kitchen; in fact, they very often communicate directly with a more formal dining room. All the gadgets and kitchen tools are unfortunately hidden behind paneled doors. In the middle of what is usually a round table may be a Murano crystal bowl probably filled with colored fruits or vegetables also made from Murano glass. In many cases these kitchens are places where food is produced more to impress than to please.

I prefer to talk about the traditional kitchens of the countryside, which offer warmth and more than a touch of nostalgia. In many of these kitchens it is still possible to find a wood- or coal-fired stove with iron cooking rings and at the side a long chrome-lidded container that contains constant hot water. The smoke pipe, which is usually painted silver, disappears into the wall. However, progress often now requires the installation of a gas or electric cooktop and oven.

In the middle of the traditional kitchen stands a rectangular table usually covered with a checked or floral wax cloth—very easy to clean— and surrounded by at least six wooden chairs with woven straw seats covered with colorful cushions. If the family has peasant origins, there will certainly be an *arca* made of walnut. This is a rectangular box with a hinged lid, which was used to hold flour and bread and also served as a seat. Standing against one of the walls is a *credenza*, a hutch (dresser), where all the tools and gadgets, pots and pans are stored. The top shelves are stacked with kitchen souvenirs, with images of the Madonna in the most prominent place.

On the wall above the stove is a shelf decorated with brightly colored paper, which will be changed at Easter, during the great spring clean, when the *credenza* also receives a new coat of paint. On the shelf are many jars, square terracotta containers for flour, sugar, salt, and coffee— the very basic ingredients of these kitchens. The sink next to the stove is made out of marble or *graniglia*, a mixture of stone and cement. Nowadays there is also a refrigerator amid all this pleasant and familiar furniture. The ambience of such kitchens is very warm, and everybody gathers round the table not only to eat but also to have a gossip with a neighbor over a cup of coffee made by a "moka express" machine.

Every family has its own preferred kitchen tools for specific dishes. In some families these cooking utensils have been handed down from generation to generation and have now become so sought after that they are real collectors' pieces. There is, for example, the *bruns* or *paiolo*, which

every real Piemontese cook owns. This is a special pan for cooking polenta, the cornmeal dish that was once the staple diet of farmers. The pan was originally made of bronze but today is more likely to be made of beaten copper. The best polenta is cooked the traditional way with the pot hanging from a chain over an open wood fire. The pot must be stirred for a good hour with a wooden spoon until the polenta comes away from the sides. It is then poured out onto a wooden board, cut with a wire, and eaten with either cheese or a meat *ragout*.

Other obligatory equipment in a Piemontese cook's room are the *pignatin* and the *duja*. The *pignatin* is a glazed earthenware pot made to accommodate a candle underneath in order to keep the *bagna cauda* warm. This is a hot dip made from anchovies and garlic into which are dipped raw and succulent pieces of pepper, cardoon, Jerusalem artichoke, fennel, and celery. The *duja* is a large terracotta pot in which cannellini beans are cooked. This was once done whenever bread was baked and the wood-fired oven was used. Today the beans are cooked on the gas stove with a wire mesh between the flame and the pot to prevent it from cracking. A different-shaped, deeper *duja* was used, and indeed still is, to store the small salamis made when the family pig was slaughtered.

Few cooks like to be left alone to get on with the chores while their guests are enjoying themselves elsewhere. The ideal kitchen plan creates a pleasant, friendly environment for all (top).

Robust fare (above) makes good use of home-cured meats and a wealth of vegetables.

A variety of specialized traditional chopping and slicing utensils is essential to the daily preparation of fresh ingredients. The *mandulin*, for example, is a flat board with a very sharp blade which can be adjusted to give thick or thin slices. It is used to shave very thin slices of the renowned white truffle from Alba onto risottos, pastas, and other dishes. (It is interesting to note that this fungus, which in some very grand delicatessens is priced at thousands of dollars per kilo, will be bought at least once a year by almost everybody, regardless of income, in order to have the sensation of this memorable food.) A knife originally used to cut hay and grass, called a *ransa*, is now much appreciated by those lucky enough still to have one. It has a wooden handle and a short razor-sharp blade made from carbon steel.

Granite, which is abundant in the mountains of the Aosta valley, is used to make mortars, instead of the marble used elsewhere in Italy. The mortar, combined with a wooden pestle, is ideal for reducing herbs such as basil, parsley, and garlic to a paste for sauces. The sauces are tasted with a wooden spoon called an *acher*, while wine is sampled with a wooden cup called a *cupet*.

Valued as much for their intrinsic beauty as their usefulness, earthenware and terracotta pots, well-worn pestles and mortars, wooden spoons, cutting boards, and knives have become collectors' items.

Among the first Europeans to drink coffee and open coffee bars, the Italians have developed a battery of equipment for making the perfect cup of espresso or caffè filtrata (drip coffee). As usual, the appearance of the utensil is considered important, as these fine copper models illustrate. A cup of friendship, the coppa dell'amicizia, is a mixture of coffee and grappa served in a grolla (grail), a multi-spouted bowl with a lid. The idea derives from the Knights of the Holy Grail who all drank from the same vessel. In the Valle d'Aosta region, grolle are fashioned from wood and carved with fruit or garlands of flowers.

Finally, particularly in the Aosta valley, the *grolla* or the *coppa dell amicizia* is to be found in every kitchen. This treacherous container with between three and eight mouthpieces is carved out of one piece of wood, usually cherrywood. It has a small lid and is made to contain coffee. It is not, however, a simple coffee, since abundant grappa and brandy will have been added to the piping-hot black liquid. On the rim of the opening some sugar moistened with grappa is lit and caramelized to give extra flavor to the mixture. This incendiary operation is performed between each tasting, and each of the guests drinks out of his or her own mouthpiece. The coppa is a symbol of friendship and, whether the kitchen is grand and ostentatious or the humble corner of a cottage, the hospitality in Piemonte is based on the warmth with which the cook prepares and serves delicious meals to her guests.

PASUS
A Basque Kitchen

❖

MARÍA JOSÉ SEVILLA-TAYLOR

Until the second half of the nineteenth century almost all the needs of the people of the rural Basque region were supplied by the economic endeavor of the individual family. The industrialization of the Basque Country saw winds of change sweep through the ancient but solid walls of the farmstead and its kitchen—the kitchen that had been the scene of and witness to every important decision and event in the life of the people who, since time immemorial, have inhabited the beautiful northeastern area of the Iberian Peninsula.

A typical example of the changing Basque kitchen is Pasus, a *caserío de montaña* or a traditional rural Basque house, built more than four hundred years ago in the Villabona district of the province of Guipuzcoa. Its roofline is irregular, its gable-ends are of differing sizes and its tiles handmade locally. The main facade, unlike more ostentatious dwellings, has no brightly colored red or green shutters, but is graced by six windows and a simple front door, which in summer is shaded by the leafy canopy of an ancient vine. To the left of the door lies the cowshed and to the right the cellar, where in winter the cider ferments. (Cider is the local drink and in this case is of excellent quality.)

The kitchen at Pasus is on the right-hand side of the building, on the ground floor. It looks out onto the women's kitchen garden. Some years ago the owner of the house decided to modernize the original kitchen and, in the name of progress, valuable antique furnishings were replaced by functional units in pale gray formica. The walls were lined with easily cleaned tiles, and the mantelpiece that adorned the great chimney-breast over the low hearth was refurbished.

Despite this modernization, some of the most traditional details of the Pasus kitchen have survived. The highly polished terracotta floor, which has withstood the tread of many generations, has been left in place and the old table still plays an important part in the daily chores. The ceiling is still painted the pale pink color that typifies houses in Basque mountain regions. The iron range, which replaced the low hearth at the beginning of the century, reigns supreme when it comes to cooking the

Caserío Pasus and part of the vegetable garden (above). Tomatoes, sweet peppers, and chilies are essential to Basque cooking. All are incorporated in bacalao a la viscaina, *a popular dish of salt cod baked in tomato and pepper sauce.*

A carved cupboard with lattice doors houses earthenware jugs and bowls (opposite).

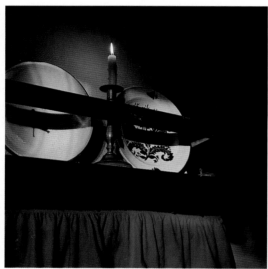

Patziyak suspended over the glowing embers (top). This cauldron could be used for boiling water or making soups. Roasted meats and baked fish dishes require a good supply of earthenware casseroles. Marmita-kua, tuna-fish steaks simmered with onions, garlic, tomatoes, sweet peppers, and potatoes, should be cooked and served in the same earthenware dish. The candle and plates (above) are typical of the region.

best stews. The only thing the newly acquired bottled-gas cooker is allowed to do is to heat the breakfast snacks and afternoon coffee.

One must admit, however, that the present-day kitchen at Pasus has lost some of its former charm and character. Though, as the old *aexoandre* (the matriarch) points out, you must look beyond the industrialization of the nineteenth century, as far back as the seventeenth century, to establish what the farmhouse kitchen was originally like. In the oldest kitchens the fireplace would have been situated in the center of the room and the smoke, with no chimney to guide it, would waft up among the roof timbers after it had lent its color to the cheeses hanging from the beams and to the odd spiced sausage or ham left from the pig-killing in the previous November.

In the original kitchen at Pasus, there was a recess in the wall with a hearth of bricks or flagstones, which formed the *suarka* (fireplace and grate). The fire was built on a cast-iron plate and behind this another sheet of metal, decorated with embossed designs and figures, formed the fireback. A firedog on either side enclosed the fire, and suspended above the grate from an iron bar across the chimney was the pot hanger. This consisted of an iron chain of some fifteen or sixteen links, about 16 inches (40 centimeters) long, with a hook on the end, to which the cauldron, or *patziyak*, was attached. The length of the chain could be adjusted to alter the distance between pot and fire. This resiting of the fireplace from the center of the room to a recess in the wall was a significant change in the history of the Basque kitchen.

The chimney-breast at Pasus was, like chimneys in other farmsteads, adorned with a piece of linen. This one was blue and white, painstakingly embroidered during the cold winter evenings—the only time when the busy farmer's wife could sit down to sew. Immediately above the piece of embroidery was a set of wooden shelves displaying a number of decorative and useful objects—plates depicting various representations of the Virgin Mary, our Lady of Aranzaza, Begoña, or Estibaliz; a copper chocolate pot; and a range of jugs. Other utensils and gadgets hung on the inside walls of the fireplace, among them the *braxera*, or chestnut roaster, and the oil lamp.

Although nowadays Pasus has two roomy stainless steel sinks and hot and cold water on demand, in the mid-nineteenth century the sink occupied a niche in the thickness of the outside wall. It was reached by two steps that also served as a plinth for the wooden pails or pitchers encircled by wooden bands, in which the water was brought from the spring each day.

Many of the original furnishings of Basque kitchens are now prized as antiques, such as the seventeenth-century cupboard of classic Basque design that once stood in the kitchen at Pasus. It had two doors above and two below, all cut from the same piece of wood, with one or two drawers halfway down. The whole piece was decorated with eight-petaled flowers and wooden beading, and was used for storing glasses and crockery. It was later replaced by a hutch (dresser), now in the dining room at Pasus,

which is possibly the oldest and most valuable piece in the house. But its value lies less in any distinctive feature than in the range of utensils that are meticulously aligned on it in perfect formation: cups, bowls, dishes, wineglasses, and tumblers, not forgetting the shiny tinware bought by a mariner ashore in the Low Countries.

A corner of the kitchen with its fireplace and cheerfully ornamented chimney-breast. Implements for spinning wool are stored above the fire.

A view of Pasus and surrounding land. The sweeping plains and foothills of Guipuzcoa extend to the snow-covered peaks of the Pyrenees, the division between France and Spain.

Originally there would have been a *txitxilu* beside the hearth. This was a high-backed wooden settle with a small board folded against it, which served as a table. The men of the house would make themselves comfortable on the bench seat, underneath which was a chest-type drawer where household linen was stored. Another folding table of well-polished wood rested on the wall. This multi-purpose table is typical of the Basque Country and can still be seen in some restaurants.

At Pasus, however, there has always been another large table near the fireplace, which is used for everyday family meals. Breakfast—just coffee or a camomile infusion—is prepared as dawn breaks. Two hours later the family gathers again around the kitchen table for a more substantial *almuerzo* of fried eggs, ham, and bread. At midday the *aexoandre* is busy cooking the main meal of the day. There is a bean stew as a first course, followed by a meat or fish dish cooked patiently in the traditional earthenware pots or *cazuelas*, as well as a salad and fresh fruit. Work in the *caserío* is extremely hard, and by five o'clock cod omelets and plates of sliced homemade *chorizo* or *salchichon* are well deserved and eagerly awaited. A light meal of soup, such as *purrusalda* (leek and potato), and bread marks the end of the day.

The *aexoandre* remembers particular utensils, some of them now sadly lost or badly worn, which her mother kept on top of the old cupboard or on one or two shelves fixed to the kitchen walls. There were large copper pans and the famous wooden utensils, some of which were unique to this country, dating back to the first inhabitants of Iberia. There would have been, for example, the *kaiku*, a wooden vessel with a handle used for milking and for making *mamia* (junket); the *oporra*, a small cup of the same shape; the *abatza*, a large wooden container for making cheese; and the *zimitza*, a wooden mold to give the cheese the desired shape and distinctive pattern.

Bread was made from maize or wheat, though the latter only once a week since a wheaten loaf, fresh from the oven, offered an irresistible and too costly temptation. The bread dough was prepared in a room reserved for this purpose, called the *maira*. At Pasus this little room was next to the kitchen, and in it was kept a most beautiful *kutxak* or chest, which was used for storing grain. The *maira* now serves as a larder where all sorts of provisions are kept: bags of potatoes, beans or lentils, flour, sugar, salt, hams and cheeses, tomato sauces, winter or summer compotes and, dominating everything, the large fridge/freezer whose presence has modified the seasonal diet to some degree.

There have been many changes in Basque rural life, and the traditional Basque kitchen lives on only in the memories of the very old, and, perhaps, in the hopes of those city dwellers who, tired of the increasing pressures and tensions of urban life, turn their gaze once again toward the mountains. These newcomers are, however, faced with a dilemma, for they must resign themselves to imitating during the weekend, in the old farmhouse they have bought or inherited, a simpler way of life that will never return.

A braxera (*chestnut roaster*) *leans against the wall* (top). *Castanea sativa, the European or Spanish chestnut, is the world's finest species. The nuts are large and sweet and are cooked with vegetables, in meat and dessert dishes. A finely carved* kutxak *used for storing grain* (above).

Wooden implements for cheesemaking (top). *Basque cheeses include Idiazabal, a hard, lightly smoked cheese made from sheep's milk. Roncal, also of sheep's milk, is a harder, smaller variety of the famous Spanish cheese Manchego, and is rich and flavorful. Kaiku* (above) *is a beautifully shaped vessel used for milking.*

THE TUSCAN KITCHEN
Simplicity and Refinement

FULVIA SESANI

Tuscany *separates the north of Italy from the south. The climate is mild and the land is rich in plants and wildlife. The countryside of this noble region is characterized by the gently rolling hills and sharp-pointed cypress trees that flank the roads leading to manorhouse and country cottage alike—the cypresses a legacy of the days when the custom was to plant a cypress every time a baby boy was born.*

A wood-fired wall oven, spartan in its simplicity (above).

Bread is a staple in the Tuscan kitchen (opposite). The round, fairly flat pane basso, *or country bread, goes hard as it turns stale and is useful as a thickening agent in soups such as* ribollita. Parmigiano *and the sheep's milk cheese* pecorino *are often used in cooking.*

The most important and most spacious room in a traditional nineteenth-century Tuscan house was the kitchen, and within the kitchen the focal point was the old stone fireplace. Through the summer people lived outside in the courtyard, but in winter they congregated in the kitchen because it was the only warm place in the house. And the best place in the kitchen was the fireplace. Here the food was cooked and the family gathered: the fireplace both sustained and maintained the group.

The fireplace was at one end of the kitchen, built on a base of stone, under which wood was stored to dry. The fire was fueled with aromatic woods and seasoned logs, the flames were kept alive with a fan of turkey feathers, and smoke was drawn up under a large hood. Around the chimney hung large gridirons on which meat was cooked in winter. (In summer it was roasted outside.) The meat was placed on the gridiron with a *leccarda*, or dripping pan, underneath to collect the juices and, with a delicate stirring motion, the *leccarda* was "licked" with a feather to produce a delicious savory sauce. The *leccarde* were made of tinned copper in a range of sizes according to whether they were for cooking large game or small birds.

When the meat was cooked the fire was allowed to die down and in the evening, on the almost extinguished charcoal, slow-cooking dishes were set to cook. The traditional *fagioli all 'uccelletto* (a bean and tomato dish which translates literally as "beans cooked in the style of little birds") was cooked in this way. The ingredients were placed in a *fiasco* (a straw-covered empty wine bottle made at the glass works in Empoli) and put on

top of the embers. In autumn the dying fire was used for roasting chestnuts. The chestnuts were cut with a *castrino*, a small curved knife, then placed in a pierced pan hanging by the fireplace.

Next to the chimney stood a wood-fired oven used for baking bread. As many farmhouses were too remote for the housewife to go to the village every day, bread was baked once a week in a quantity large enough to last the whole week. Farmhouse Tuscan bread was called *sciocco*, or "stupid," because it had no salt. There were two reasons for this: firstly, the bread kept longer without salt; and, secondly, salt was very expensive and was, in fact, used as a trading commodity.

Near the oven, against the wall, was a *madia*, a low piece of furniture rather like a chest, with a hinged lid that opened upward. It was used for storing flour and bread, and was common throughout northern Italy. The best pieces were made of finely carved walnut but even when a less precious wood was used, the *madia*, like other kitchen furniture, was always well made and chosen with care.

Centrally positioned and facing each other against opposite kitchen walls were two *credenze* or (hutches) dressers. The Italian name derives from *far credenza*, the verb meaning "to have trust in" or "believe." In the past the landholder, who was always afraid of being poisoned, demanded that his servants taste his food first. They did this leaning on the hutch (dresser) and thus its name evolved.

On the top of the *credenza* was a glass-fronted cabinet in which candelabra and oil lamps were kept. Below was a cupboard for storing plates, soup tureens, and salad bowls. Above the cupboard was a cutlery drawer topped with a large marble slab on which food and plates were placed. The family took their meals around a big table made of solid wood, generally oak, that dominated the middle of the kitchen.

Large shelves on the walls of the kitchen displayed the cooking pots and pans: shiny copper pans of various shapes and sizes; large and small saucepans for frying or sautéing meat, fish, and vegetables; and earthenware pots for slow-cooking soups such as *ribollita* (literally, reboiled) soup—an old country recipe for a soup made with vegetables and stale bread, which was made the day before it was to be served, then reheated while awaiting the return of the men from the fields.

Hanging on the wall was a knife rack. In Tuscany there is a strong tradition of game cookery and a wealth of imaginative ways for preparing it (just think, for example, of the *dolceforte*—sweet and spicy wild boar with a sauce of vinegar and bitter chocolate). It was natural, therefore, that knives had a place of honor in the kitchen, with a selection of different sizes and shapes for dividing, cutting, dressing, filleting, and slicing the meat.

The large rectangular kitchen sink was made from a single piece of locally quarried marble. Before the advent of a piped water supply water was drawn fresh from a well in the courtyard, overlooked by the kitchen. Just outside the door to the yard, the housewife grew the aromatic herbs she used for flavoring the classic regional dishes: basil, thyme, marjoram,

Two traditional kitchen implements. An ornately decorated butter stamp (top), and (above) an olive press used in the production of the heavy, fruity, and richly flavored olive oils preferred in Tuscan cooking.

and rosemary. Fennel, another essential ingredient, grew wild. *Finocchiona*, an exquisite salami, took its name from the fennel seeds that gave it its characteristic flavor. Because of the strong taste and aroma of fennel seeds, it was a tradition to offer *finocchiona* to wine buyers when there had been a bad year to cover the taste of a medium quality product. This practice was called *infinocchiare*, to cheat or take in.

Tuscan cookery has always followed the seasons, and the wonderful fresh ingredients have the flavor of the woods and the plants growing wild in the hills. In autumn wild boar was hunted in the oak woods, while hare, pheasant, wild duck, woodcock, and snipe were driven out of the bushes. Olives were harvested to produce the high-quality olive oil used in traditional dishes. With the first rains fungi, such as the *porcini* and the *ovuli* (so called for their egg shape), sprouted in the undergrowth, as did the *cocchi*, an exquisite gift of nature enjoyed sliced raw, in soups, in rice dishes, and, like almost every other food in Tuscany, grilled. With the first cold days of winter, the family pig was slaughtered and preserved in salamis and many other pork dishes. In spring the fertile soil again began to produce tender and tasty vegetables.

The foods are fresh, the wines good, and the cooking, like the kitchen, is at once simple and refined.

No recipe was complete without the addition of herbs, and each housewife grew her own supply. Her kitchen was enviably functional in its design. The spacious rectangular sink, sadly no longer the norm in modern-day kitchens, was made from a single piece of marble. A simple rack above the sink kept pans tidily out of the way until needed.

Two Greek Kitchens
A Contrast in Styles

R ENA S ALAMAN

A well-appointed fitted kitchen with wood and marble detailing provides ample storage space (top). The tiled floor is both cool and easy to maintain. The smallest of cook tops (above) is fueled by a gas cylinder.

A kitchen corner in a small rural house on the island of Paros (opposite).

I *was brought up in a primitive traditional kitchen: not in a little Aegean island nor in a small mountain village, but in an Athenian suburb in the late 1940s.*

Although our city kitchen was extremely small, everything had its place. Along one wall were built-in wood-fired ranges of different sizes with a vast cauldron for washing clothes at the very end. Above it, menacingly black, loomed a huge hood-cum-chimney. On the side wall by the cooking surfaces hung two or three large blackened frying pans and various sizes of equally blackened saucepans. Adjacent to this and at a right angle to the wall was a huge, chipped marble sink, underneath which were stored two slim terracotta urns filled with water. The urns traditionally came from the nearby island of Aegena, and were famed for their cooling properties. Next to the kitchen sink was a door to the small back garden, where in summer meals were served in the shade of the ubiquitous vine. All kitchen activities took place here too, from vegetable peeling and pan cleaning to the slaughtering of the Pascal lamb.

Opposite the sink, and in pride of place, there were pretty wooden shelves fitted to the wall, which displayed—Welsh-dresser (hutch) style—a concoction of gleaming round oven pans, handmade from thick copper. These were used to carry food that had to be baked or roasted to the local baker: our ranges did not include the luxury of an oven. Opposite the ranges were built-in units with large drawers underneath for cutlery, kitchen implements and linen, and dainty cupboards on top with mesh doors for food storage (this was before we had a refrigerator). The row ended with a little glass-fronted cupboard filled with spice jars, olive oil, mustard, the ever-popular herbs—oregano and thyme—and various tisanes, all hand-picked from field and hillside.

Through an arch at one end of the kitchen was a small raised area which contained the dining table and chairs. This was where the family ate in winter. For formal occasions and large family celebrations meals were served at the large table in the front living room, which otherwise resembled a museum piece.

The local bakers of the day were themselves primitively equipped. Their cavernous ovens were wood-fired, which gave bread and roasted food a deliciously earthy aroma and unparalleled crunch, though this occasionally got out of hand and ended up with the food a little too crunchy and the loaves with scorched black corners.

Progress and modernization arrived in our suburb hand-in-hand in the shape of a gleaming electric oven installed by one of the bakers. This was called a German oven and probably literally was one. From then on the baker was nicknamed "German." People were impressed, they considered the electric oven cleaner, and the baker flourished. That was the beginning of the end as more bakers followed in his footsteps until none of the wonderful wood-fired ovens was left.

However, the tradition of each household taking its roasts to the local baker early in the morning to be baked after the bread survived and, in fact, is still going strong. Even in large cities like Athens, you can often see old ladies carrying round aluminum pans filled with spectacular contents that exude the most titillating garlic and lemon aromas, the scarlet of the tomatoes juxtaposed with the bright green of the stuffed peppers and the dark purple of the slim eggplants. Lunchtime at the local baker is one of the most exhilarating spectacles for the food lover. Resting on the large wooden or marble counters, ready for collection, is a wealth of dishes with an astounding variety of textures and colors: a golden pie; a small leg of kid surrounded by tiny pasta shapes and fresh tomatoes; a whole chicken circled with okra; a *briami* (baked zucchini, potatoes, and tomatoes); a golden-crusted *moussaka*; a *gratin* of eggplant and tomatoes. The atmosphere is thick with wonderful scents: the smell of the freshly baked bread mingles with the mouth-watering confections on the counter, the garlic, the mountainside marjoram and thyme.

A cool, white kitchen opens onto a sun-filled garden area where the cook has easy access to a home-grown supply of herbs and lemons. There can be few cooks in Greece able to survive without lemons, which, alongside another fruit—olives— are essential to Greek cuisine. The juice is used in seafood, lamb and marinated vegetable dishes, in sauces and soups, and in desserts. The rind is preserved in a thick syrup.

In my childhood home, empress of the kitchen and mistress of ceremonies was my extremely able and high-spirited grandmother. She was also one of the best cooks I have ever known. My earliest memories portray her as a kind of Cinderella, always enfolded in ashes, her gray attire uncannily matching her surroundings.

Pulses were the staple food of Greece after the war, and the slow cooking they required was perfectly suited to the wood-fired ranges. The chickpea soup, *revithia soupa*, was put on the fire the night before, on whatever life the ashes could sustain. By next morning it was thick and nourishing, and was often served to the men of the family as a substantial breakfast before they left for work.

In the late 1940s, at about the same time as the bakers were transforming themselves, the primus stove made its grand appearance in our households. These small and light brass contraptions exhibited an oversized belly resting on dwarf legs, an image that uniquely identifies the period. Their belly was the container for paraffin; you fed the belly and got fire in return. They were almost effortless to run compared with the physical demands of the huge hearth. They were also much cleaner as they left no residue, and they were easily regulated within seconds.

Family mementos, embroidery, and a display of china plates contribute to the cosy clutter of this sitting room adjacent to the kitchen.

Traditional embroidered trims soften the sparse utilitarianism of this simple kitchen.

Of course they had their drawbacks. They could accommodate only one pot at a time and they would smoke profusely and smell unpleasantly if blocked. They then had to be taken to pieces and have their parts cleaned with spirit—a performance at which my grandmother again became an ace. Occasionally they would burst into flames, then people would throw them into the garden or out of open windows to avoid setting their homes on fire. And sometimes they would even explode.

Since the original ranges doubled up as a heater for most parts of the house, the primus stove had to take over that role as well. Often on cold days people sat in the kitchen with the primus stove lit and a saucepan of water bubbling on top until late in the night.

In the late 1960s I went to the beautiful Aegean island of Alonnisos in the Sporades. With its tranquil harbor reflecting the white of the houses and the green of the trees, it seemed almost unreal. Up on the far hill was a cluster of little white cubes. This was the original old village, parts of which date back to the thirteenth century. Life there seemed to have stood still for at least a hundred years. Each household was largely self-sufficient, relying only on friends and relations for certain provisions and services. All the families cultivated their own vegetables and owned their own chicken and at least two or three goats. So eggs, milk, cheese, and yogurt were available in each household.

The typical design of the stone houses was "one up, one down." The "down" room was the heart of the household: the center for family activity. It was dominated in one corner by a huge but handsome hearth covered by a smooth, circular apron that reached the ceiling like a cone. In the wall at the back of the fireplace was a semicircular opening into a built-in oven—a necessity since the luxury of the city baker was unheard of in such a primitive place. This structure, so simple and unadorned, was to impress me more than any other cooking device I had ever experienced. Ovens in general are a special enthusiasm of mine, as I think some of the simplest dishes can be transformed by baking or roasting and I like to imagine the excitement of the first cook who discovered, perhaps accidentally, what could be done with a vegetable by burying it in the ashes instead of boiling it.

For the Alonnisian cook, this was a standard part of the kitchen area, quite unlike the city cook's room. If the peasant kitchen was matched against the city one, it scored on every front: in aspects of design as well as in the results of its cooking.

Let me describe this room that contained the whole family and its daily activities. It was quite large, square and open, often with a dark, cool, rocky area leading from it. The huge terracotta jars, *pytharia*, that

Blue and white accessories echo the white buildings and blue skies beyond the confines of this Greek island home.

Easter Sunday is a day for great celebration in Greece, and food preparation gets underway well in advance. Dozens of eggs are dyed bright red (the color of blood and victory) and polished with olive oil. They are used in the ritual Easter Sunday game of who can crack whose egg. Tsoureki, a rich Easter bread, is made (above and opposite); it is often flavored with machlepi, *a herb with a strong taste resembling aniseed. The loaves are plaited or shaped into rounds and may be decorated with red eggs before baking.*

stored the family-produced olive oil were kept here. Life revolved around the corner hearth. As there was no electricity, the wood fire provided not only heat for cooking but also a central light. The upstairs was reached by a wooden staircase leading from one side of the room, usually opposite the front door. Against and underneath this staircase the kitchen implements were stored either on shelves or on hooks. Pride of place was given to the large round copper baking pans which, like the *pytharia*, were passed from mother to daughter as part of her dowry. Here, too, blackened saucepans, a frying pan or two, a wooden pestle and mortar, and various other small utensils were kept. Larger implements were stored horizontally on the sturdy beams that crossed the length of the ceiling. The bread stick, for example, was stored here. This had a long wooden handle with a flat square end like a hand, and was used for depositing each loaf and each baking pan into the oven.

As I got to know the people on Alonnisos and eventually bought a house there, I also became familiar with their cooking methods. One of the families I became very close to were our neighbors, the Karakatsanis. The matriarch of the family, Kyria Maria, was a magnificent cook, weaver and lacemaker, and displayed many other talents which the women of the countryside seem to hold so lightly. The hearth fire needed confident and dextrous handling, gained through years of experience: Kyria Maria performed magic with her home hearth.

She lit the fire with sticks, left it to die down a little, and placed an iron tripod over it with a saucepan resting on the tripod. Then she started her cooking: perhaps a frugal casserole of beans followed by some crisply fried tiny fish or squid that her brother-in-law, a fisherman, had sent that morning. But the most astounding cooking was reserved for celebrations, when elaborate pies with all kinds of fresh wild greens collected from the hillside were baked, or a chicken, surrounded by potatoes and dressed with lemon juice and thyme, was roasted to perfection in half the time it would take in a conventional oven. Kyria Maria placed a large pile of sticks into the oven at the back of the hearth and lit them. At just the right moment, when the fierce flame had dwindled to a glow, she raked the sticks out, to be used for the remaining cooking. By then the oven was fiery hot, the dish to be baked was placed inside, and the opening sealed with a metal sheet.

Some houses had an outdoor oven, shaped like a beehive. This was used in the summer when cooking inside, was unbearably hot. We learned that particular ovens had particular qualities. Our courtyard oven, for example, was famed in the village for baking the most delicious bread. In order to make the most efficient use of the lit ovens, bread was baked communally among friends. Bread day was a festive day, with the whole neighborhood in commotion from dawn onward.

But this is an endless story of miraculous results from primitive means: a way of life that now seems utopian compared with our modern microwaves and electrical gadgets; a dream of escape, perhaps, like our summer home on the island.

NORTH, CENTRAL, & SOUTH AMERICA

❖

The Mexican Kitchen   Chesapeake   Kitchens in Seattle
Canada   The First Kitchen   Peru

THE MEXICAN KITCHEN
A Legacy of Spain

❖

D I A N A   S O U T H W O O D   K E N N E D Y

The traditional Mexican kitchen, as we imagine it today, dates back to the earliest years of the Spanish colonial era in the first half of the sixteenth century, although many of the utensils, ingredients, and cooking methods actually predate the Spanish conquest. Our only images of early kitchens are those depicted in genre paintings from the seventeenth to the early part of the twentieth centuries. To my knowledge, no book about the architecture of those times dwells at length on the subject of kitchens.

The first colonial kitchens were undoubtedly those of the convents and monasteries, followed closely by those in the palaces of the Spanish grandees. The convent kitchens were great cavernous places designed to feed large numbers, not only of their fraternities but also of visitors seeking refuge in an alien land. One complete length of wall was given over to a massive fireplace where meats were roasted on spits and pots of food cooked in the hot embers. There would most certainly have been a large bread oven, alcoves for storing the cooking utensils, and rough wooden workbenches. By the eighteenth century, the convent kitchens of Puebla and Tlaxcala were decorated with multicolored tiles.

As the Spaniards fanned out across the country, haciendas were established. Their kitchens, while still having to cater to large numbers, were gradually modified and became more sophisticated. A series of fireboxes was strung along a wall that was vented at the top, with a separate, larger fire to accommodate the round unglazed earthenware "bakestone," or *comal*, used for cooking tortillas. The women who made them knelt on the floor in front of their volcanic rock grinding stones (*metates*), and ground the prepared corn into a soft dough. As the tortillas were patted out, cooked, and puffed up they were kept warm in reed or palm baskets, or, in the hotter climates, in hollowed-out gourds. Tortillas were a staple of pre-Columbian Mexico and are still, especially in the country areas, the most important basic foodstuff.

These kitchens are remarkable for the juxtaposition of glazed and matt surfaces, pale and vibrant tones, patterns and plains.

124

The versatile tortilla is unusual among breads in that it is made from cooked, not raw, flour. Dried corn is boiled in limewater until the skin on the kernels loosens. The cooked, skinned kernels are then dried and ground on a stone (metate) and mixed with water to make a soft dough (masa). The dough is pressed on an appliance designed for the purpose or patted into shape by hand; the unbaked tortillas are about 8 inches (20 centime-ters) in diameter and an eighth of an inch (3 millimeters) thick. The cooking time on an ungreased earthenware griddle (comal) is brief. Tortillas are always eaten warm or hot, either on their own as bread, or prepared in a variety of ways with fillings and spicy sauces in which chilies frequently are included. The spices are ground in a stone mortar (molcajete). Of about two hundred types of chili, about half find their way into Mexican cooking in fresh or dried form. Of the red varieties, guajillo is among the hottest, while cascabel is plumper and less fierce on the palate.

In vibrant surroundings, tradition and modernity coexist (opposite).

There was a proliferation of earthenware pots, and stone and wooden implements in the traditional kitchen. The vast pots were used to hold grains or water. Spoons and other essentials were stored in a carved wooden stand (cucharera) that hung on the wall.

In the traditional kitchen there were *fresqueras*, slatted shelves for storing foods, that were hoisted up out of reach of passing marauders. There were many large earthenware containers for water or grains, and most certainly a carved wooden *cucharera* hanging on the wall for holding spoons, chocolate beaters, and wooden paddles for stirring deep pots. (A particularly lovely one is on view in the kitchen of the Santa Rosa Convent in Puebla, and very decorative ones made of pine are still made by local craftsmen in the Michoacán highlands.)

Walls were constructed of adobe brick: clay bonded with straw or tough dried grasses, compressed into rectangular brick shapes, then sun-dried. These were often charmingly decorated in abstract patterns, with strings of earthenware mugs, pots, or little casseroles (*cazuelas*) in graduating sizes hanging on small metal hooks. The most primitive floors were of earth beaten down until compressed to a hard, smooth surface; others were covered with large unglazed earthenware tiles.

In design and concept, many of the utensils of the early Spanish kitchen dated from pre-Columbian times. In fact they are still made in the same forms and sold in markets throughout Mexico: earthenware "bakestones," stone mortars (*molcajetes*) and pestles (*tejolotes*), grinding stones and their mullers (*manos*), earthenware pots, jugs and casseroles, and small palm fans (*sopladores*) to stir up a sullen fire. From archeological sites we know that cooking was done either on a hearth on the floor, on braziers, or in pits in the ground. There were ovens, but they were used as steam baths (*temascales*), mostly for ritual cleansings.

Today in remote rural areas of Mexico you can still find simple but functional kitchens made of basic local materials. Sheltered by palm—thatch roofs, they are set apart from the main dwelling area. The walls are made either of a kind of daub and wattle, or thick reeds or bamboo for better ventilation in the hotter climates, and the floors are of compacted earth. The stove (*bracero*) is a baked clay construction—sometimes reinforced with a little cement—supported at a good working level by the stout trunks of tropical hardwoods. I have often marveled at the ingenuity of design and innovation that fulfills the needs of the cook and suits the sizes and types of pots she uses. In the hot country of Michoacán I have seen a kitchen built around a huge tree trunk that made a perfect hutch (dresser) for hanging all types of kitchen utensils. Again, there is always a separate area for making tortillas with the *comal* fitted into the base construction just above the fire and at a convenient height for the tortilla maker to work.

In the 1950s and 1960s it was fashionable among some well-to-do Mexicans, and even more among foreign residents, to build pseudo-colonial houses that included quite charming kitchens decorated with brightly colored tiles and with decidedly traditional elements incorporated into their design. But as the urban centers in Mexico burgeoned and apartment living became the rule rather than the exception, kitchens tended to become more functional, colder, and more impersonal. Yet if you look carefully around a modern kitchen you can always find a small battered tin *comal*, a well-ground *molcajete* redolent of past sauces, and perhaps a small tortilla basket tucked away between the bright blue enameled pots—hallmarks of modern Mexican kitchen equipment—the blender, and the pressure cooker. Whether they belonged to the mistress of the house or were brought in by the maid from her family home matters little; they are there and in use.

I have tried to incorporate as many traditional features as possible into my own kitchen, not only because they are particularly appropriate here in the Michoacán countryside, but also because I love the solid earthy quality of both the local building materials and the earthenware pots and stone implements. Apart from their aesthetic appeal, I truly believe that these utensils impart a very special quality to the food.

In fact, I have two kitchens: one inside and more conventional, and the other out in the open air on a naturally formed terrace that extends beyond the main kitchen wall. The latter is an L-shaped construction of adobe bricks finished with a thin slurry of earth and cement tinted with a terracotta-colored paint. An arched alcove at the end holds kindling and firewood, and along the cooking "counter" are four fire-boxes: one hooded for grilling; a large circular one for the clay *comal*; and two smaller spaces into which round-bottomed earthenware pots (*ollas*) can be held firmly above the fire. Adjoining this structure and to the right are two beehive-

Walls are often decorated with platters, bowls, and jugs of all proportions. Rich earthy colors and brilliant yellows and blues predominate.

Looking more like a piece of sculpture than a cooking appliance, this terracotta-pink bread oven (top) is one of two situated outdoors near the author's main kitchen. The curved cooking-cum-work station (above) dominates the main kitchen. The vitality of its covering of blue and white tiles contrasts with the unglazed clay floor.

shaped ovens also made of round-sided adobe bricks specially formed for this type of construction. They are typical of the wood fired bread ovens used by the bakers in this area and, incidentally, for cooking *barbacoa*, lamb or goat wrapped in the fleshy leaves of the maguey plant. In the same terrace area and to one side of the ovens is a brick-lined pit designed to emulate the cooking of the pit-barbecues practiced in the neighboring highland areas.

The walls of the inside kitchen are of adobe brick and painted a deep earthy red, and the floor is tiled with large squares of unglazed clay. The ceiling is also of unglazed tiles, smaller and mottled pinkish in color, and supported by transverse beams of cedar and pine. The cupboards and drawers were made from old cedar doors rescued—as was the ceiling material—from demolition sites in the nearby town.

The main feature of my kitchen-cum-dining room is a massive cooking "peninsula" jutting out from a natural rockface that forms part of the west wall. It is a solid construction of adobe bricks with a small arch running through from one side to the other to stow away the large earthenware containers that contain dry dog-food or the parched corn kernels waiting to be transformed into dough for tortillas. The sides of the stove are faced with blue and white patterned tiles—copies of those used in a Morelia kitchen (Morelia is the capital of the state of Michoacán) possibly three centuries ago, and made in a village nearby. Gas burners of different dimensions—with a very large one for the *comal*—are set around the edge, and what remains of the surface space is always full of kitchen paraphernalia: whisks, thermometers, wooden spoons, spatulas, and scrapers held upright in earthenware jugs or wire egg baskets.

The expanse of windows that forms the east wall of the kitchen, overlooking the terrace area, is relieved by a stout wooden bar from which hang baskets of various sizes and forms. They are not there just for decoration but are in constant use for storing an overflow of dried chilies and, of course, for marketing. On the long counter below the windows sits a large, hand-hammered, copper stockpot generally given over to the storage of a year's supply of sugar-cones from the primitive mill in the canefields less than an hour's drive away. There are fermenting flagons of pineapple and banana vinegars, a clay lamb coated with a green fuzz of sprouted *chia* seeds, a grain mill, an antique coffee roaster, and a bright red scale that weighs down to 5 grams with accuracy. Rustic wooden trays (*bateas*) hold fruit and vegetables, while two large unglazed earthenware jugs keep the boiled drinking water cool.

The north wall of the kitchen is painted a deep red, and hung on it around the black metal stove (for heating) is copperware from France and Portugal, with pride of place reserved for the unlined copper preserving pans (*cazos*) used throughout central Mexico—and particularly in Michoacán where they are made—for fruit preserves, jams, and pastes. Their design dates back well into the colonial period when Don Vasco de Quiroga introduced new crafts to the villages of the Tarascan highlands

around Lake Patzcuaro. The working of copper fell to Santa Clara de Cobre, where it is still a thriving industry.

To one side of the copperware on the same wall is a false alcove with antique pine beams as shelves. It is ideal for displaying a large part of my collection of earthenware cooking pots and jugs from many parts of Mexico. An antique pine hutch (dresser) from the Patzcuaro area displays smaller plates and jugs, the majority made in the craft villages of Michoacán. Below, earthenware containers store green coffee beans from the orchard. The entrance to the kitchen is adorned by a large hemp sling (*huangoche*) spilling over with kitchen miscellanea: dried corn husks, wooden cheese hoops, branches of bay, and decorative palm weavings from the previous Easter week celebrations, all very much a part of the traditional Mexican kitchen.

But there is one important thing missing from my kitchen: a portrait—oil painting or tiled—of the patron saint of the Mexican kitchen, San Pascual Bailón, a cult figure of the eighteenth century created in the convents of Puebla. But I don't know where I would put him: hanging him from the ceiling would hardly be appropriate!

Gloriously colored fungi, chilies, and squash blossoms (above left). In the background, the author sets to work.

A glut of fruit (top) is easily turned into many months' supply of preserves, jams, and pastes.

A traditional hutch (dresser) from the Patzcuaro area (above).

CHESAPEAKE
Colonial Family Kitchens

W ILLIE G RAHAM

*The meat safe, made of wood and hessian
(above), kept food cool before refrigeration
became widely available.*

*Chairs with straight back-posts and rush seats
were common throughout the early colonial period
(opposite). Tables were often set with
pewterware, vast quantities of which were shipped
from England during the eighteenth century.*

Early in the history of the Chesapeake region of Virginia,
cooking took place within the house much like elsewhere in the colonies.
During the late seventeenth century most houses had just one or two rooms
and it was the hall—whether in a one- or multi-room dwelling—that most
often served the combined functions of living, dining, sleeping, and cooking.

By the eighteenth century, with increasing concerns for privacy and a
greater need for entertaining, houses took on new forms. However for
many, mostly those who were poor or black, the hall house (with one room
below and a chamber in the loft) continued to be used at least until the
time of the American Civil War. A traveler in 1780 noted "here and
there in the woods we saw Virginia cabins, built of unhewn logs and
without windows. Kitchen, living room, bed room and hall are all in one
room into which one enters when the house door opens."

By this time, Chesapeake architecture had developed quite distinctly
from that of New England and the mother country. Several factors caused
this distinction, not the least of which were responses to environmental
and social concerns. What became the norm in Maryland and Virginia,
at least for those above the middling range, was a fairly small house with
a separate kitchen and service buildings. If one owned slaves, detached
work areas allowed for social segregation, while for those without
servants, there was at least a clear division between the living and the
work spaces. The detached kitchen became a conspicuous feature of the
Tidewater landscape.

The eighteenth-century kitchen became, at least symbolically, the
point of interaction between the blacks and whites who shared the site.
Servants increasingly participated in the preparation of food while at the
same time there was a tendency to move them out of view of the public
realm of the house. It was still the wife's role at least to oversee the
cooking, so she spent much of her time in the kitchen with her slaves.

As the dinner became more ostentatious and complicated, some planters felt it necessary to hire cooks with formal training. Thomas Jefferson, for instance, took his slave James Hemmings with him to France for culinary education. Yet for most, the wife or slave made do with the increasingly popular cookbook to guide them through the elaborate preparation of meals.

Just as the training a cook received reflected the planter's social status, so did the appearance of his kitchen. Toward the middle of the century, large two-storey dependencies were being included in the formal planning of the great aristocratic estates and as part of the decorative scheme for the large townhouses of the elite, such as was designed by William Buckland at the Hammond-Harwood House in Annapolis, Maryland. Yet at the same time one might find a small and primitive earth-fast structure with a wooden chimney and dirt floor belonging to a modest farmer.

In farms of any size, there was a clear relationship between the kitchen, house, and other dependencies on the property. Next to the main house and possibly the dairy, the kitchen most often was the best finished outbuilding and the most closely linked to the main dwelling.

How well fitted the kitchen was depended on the means of the owner, the time it was built and, particularly in the nineteenth century, whether it was for a town or country house. In the eighteenth century, because little movable furniture was used, at least some shelving and hutches (dressers) were needed in a smoothly run kitchen. The shelves were simple boards on brackets and the hutch (dresser) was a large plank set on a secure base. This is in contrast to the much more elaborate Welsh dressers used in English houses at this time.

From surviving buildings, a clearer picture emerges of the range of finishes used on the interior. The Council kitchen recently discovered in Southampton County, Virginia, is a round-log building with riven strips of wood nailed across the joints between each log to reduce the draft in winter. A wooden hood covered with riven clapboards served as the chimney, and large gaps between some of the boards guaranteed that the room would be filled with smoke and grease. The logs were exposed on the interior, including the ceiling joists.

The chimney-hood extended across the full width of the building. On the walls inside the fireplace were nailed several wooden hooks on which pots and pans could be stored. Opposite the fireplace end of the room were shelves and hutches (dressers), created by placing boards on long pegs that had been let into the log walls.

The cook on the Council farm had to work in a dark, grimy space. One door and two extremely small, shuttered windows provided the only light and ventilation. The cook, though, was able to keep order in this otherwise poor environment. As well as the hooks and shelves for storing kitchen utensils and the hutch (dresser) on which the food was prepared, a large, brick-lined root cellar in front of the hearth was used for the storage of vegetables. The cellar was an excavated hole, perhaps 3 feet (1 meter)

A cream teapot from Poplar Hall, Dover, Delaware, and a wine rack from the Hammond-Harwood House, Annapolis, Maryland.

deep. The floorboards were laid loosely over the hole and when access was necessary, were temporarily pulled away. The vegetables stored in the cellar were probably placed directly on the ground, much as farmers still do in southside Virginia.

In contrast to the Council kitchen, the building behind Stirling Castle in Petersburg is much better built and is representative of nineteenth-century urban design. It was built in about 1840 for John Fitzhugh May, a federal judge and local land speculator. Constructed of brick, there were two rooms on the ground floor: one for cooking and one that served as a servants' hall. The walls and ceiling of the cooking room were plastered and whitewashed, and the space was lit with three large glazed windows. Several built-in heart-pine shelves and a freestanding shelving unit supplied ample space for storing cooking utensils. Further

The elegant dining table and chairs at Poplar Hall, Dover, Delaware, illustrate the respect American furniture makers held for the natural qualities of wood. Symmetry and proportion were valued more than external decoration.

The rudimentary design of the Council kitchen, Southampton County, Virginia (above), *afforded the cook little access to light and ventilation.*

Dairy outhouses at Mattox Farm, Somerset County, Maryland (right). *The building in the background dates to the early nineteenth century; that in the foreground is from about 1840.*

storage space was provided by a closet or pantry. A wrought-iron crane on which cooking pots could be hung over the fire was installed in the fireplace. The vertical arm of the crane could be swung, making it easier to move the pot over or away from the fire. In the largest of kitchens, a fireplace might have two cranes in operation. For most, though, one crane was a luxury.

Most kitchens did not have an oven. Baked goods were either bought or prepared over the open hearth. If there was an oven, it would usually be built into the same chimney as the fireplace, adjacent to the fire-box. All the cooking was done in the inner chamber. The pre-chamber merely served as a flue for what smoke and heat might escape the door to the inner chamber.

Tables, or for that matter any kind of movable furniture, were rare in colonial kitchens. The cook had to stand at the hutch (dresser) to prepare food and kneel at the hearth to cook it. Tables did not become commonplace in kitchens until the end of the eighteenth century, when

they replaced the hutch (dresser). They were utilitarian and rather plain, made of sturdy heart-pine or tulip poplar.

After the American Revolution, most planters' and merchants' kitchens were supplied not only with tables, but with a full range of specialized items. Many of the larger and more expensive pieces had earlier been purchased from outside the region but the smaller and more ephemeral objects were undoubtedly locally crafted. As a result of the increase in specialization early in the nineteenth century and the newly available mass-produced items, the middle class was able to acquire many utensils not available even to the gentry half a century earlier. These articles were available from a wide variety of sources and brought more uniformity to American kitchens. They included such devices as ice-cream freezers, refrigerators, coolers, and cook stoves.

In Petersburg, the first mention of a refrigerator or freezer is in 1816. By 1840 virtually half of all the households listed had one or the other and it is interesting that the refrigerator was kept in the dining room,

Shirley kitchen, Charles City County, Virginia, about 1770. The oven is on the left, the cooking fireplace to the right. Kitchen tables were not the norm until the end of the eighteenth century; before then, the cook stood at a hutch (dresser) to prepare food.

Two early Chesapeake buildings. The Cibula slave quarter, Prince George County, Virginia (top). This building housed a slave family; the fire heated the building and cooked the family's food. A typical one-roomed house in Westmoreland County, Virginia (above) dating from the last quarter of the eighteenth century.

An imposing storage cupboard at the Hammond-Harwood House, Annapolis, Maryland, houses the family plate and ceramics (opposite).

not the kitchen. This location fitted well with the redesignating of the role of the dining room, where, possibly as a status symbol, the refrigerator could be viewed by guests.

Of the new equipment, it was the cook stove that eventually made the most profound change in the kitchen, though to begin with it was used only as a supplement to the traditional hearth. Cook stoves were referred to as "stoves for preserving" and were used in the canning of food but were not much more than a novelty item during the antebellum period. It was not until after the Civil War that Marylanders and Virginians acquired a taste for the overcooked food—now a stereotypical southern cuisine—that was prepared on these stoves. It was the stove, along with the abolition of slavery and the pressures of urban living, that brought about the reintegration of the kitchen into the main house.

The transformation taking place in the kitchen paralleled the changes occurring in the meal itself. During the seventeenth century, Tidewater families ate a one-pot meal. Little ritual surrounded this event: diners shared a common bench, a common drinking vessel, and ate out of a common pot. At the end of the colonial period, eating had become the focus of entertainment in America and what had earlier been a shared event became quite specialized and individualized.

In the eighteenth and nineteenth centuries, food fashion in the Chesapeake followed that in London, modified according to what produce was available in the regions, and supplemented by the abundance of native foods. A planter's wife might provide cakes, apples, oranges, figs, raisins, and almonds at a tea, and serve ham and a local dish made of Indian corn at supper.

Despite the complexities of nineteenth-century life, however, the patterns established in the last quarter of the eighteenth century still held true for most white Virginians at the time of the Civil War. Most cooked on open hearths in kitchens detached from the main house. The reasons for having segregated kitchens had also changed little. If anything, this tradition and its logic were more deeply ingrained. It became essential, as the white slave owner saw it, to organize his environment in a manner that not only separated work space and servants' housing from his main living area but also reduced the visibility of his slaves. In the twenty-five years that followed the war, many changes had to occur, forced in large part by the changing social and legal status of blacks.

On the other hand, few blacks in the Chesapeake were afforded the luxury of a separate kitchen. Slaves typically slept, ate, and worked in a single space and few free blacks could afford much better. Along with the newly established freedom for blacks in 1865 came a dynamic change in the way Southerners—and particularly those living in the Chesapeake—socialized, worked, and prepared their meals. Forced to modernize, white planters and merchants drew the kitchen back into the house. Blacks gained their freedom and thereby took more control over their living and work environments.

KITCHENS IN SEATTLE
The Pacific Northwest

S HIRLEY C OLLINS

In an area such as Seattle in the Pacific northwestern corner of the United States, culinary history is relatively short and can be traced through conveniently discernible growth rings.

Western exploration began here in the 1770s and cooking vessels from British ships soon became the most coveted of trade goods among the Indians. Cast-iron kettles, for example, replaced Indian vessels of hollowed stone, cooking pouches of woven cedar bark, and wooden cooking boxes. The latter were used to steam food by throwing hot rocks from the fire into the box which contained food and water.

By 1830 a Hudsons Bay Trading Post had been established at Fort Vancouver to serve the settlers. Among its many stocks were nursery trees. Those who had traveled an impossible distance from their homes reached for the familiar—and planted fruit trees. Many old Seattle neighborhoods are virtually orchards and their history is reflected in the well-used apple corers, cherry pitters, jam kettles, and preserving equipment: essential utensils to cater for an early and continuing love of fruit in pies and pastries, jams and jellies and, more recently, sauces.

Kitchens in Seattle have always been shaped by local fuel resources. When the heavily wooded slopes of Elliott Bay were being cleared in the 1850s, wood was the obvious choice for fuel, and several stove and range manufacturers are to be found in the early lists of local industries. Within decades, heavy coal deposits were opened in an area 20 miles (32 kilometers) to the south and east of Seattle, and a rail line was built from the pits to the docks, from which ships carried coal to San Francisco. Coal was soon used in the ranges as it burned longer and hotter and was effective in banking down the wood fires overnight.

The coal and wood range was the center of the house and its most important piece of equipment. Big and cumbersome, it was often very beautifully decorated with nickel embellishments. A fire-box to one side held the coal and wood; directly above it was the flue. When the damper on the side of the fire-box was closed, the flame was directed into the area

Constance Wiggins Crookham at work in her kitchen in Oregon (above). It boasts cast-iron utensils and an adequate source of natural light. Though modest in its appointments by today's standards, it was functional and efficient to run.

The gleaming ranges (opposite) which, unlike earlier models, now operate on a variety of energy resources, have been "rediscovered" in the latter part of the twentieth century. They are appreciated for the flexibility they afford the cook and their usefulness as a source of heating.

The importance of wood as a building material is well illustrated in this photograph of a kitchen corner, taken in a Burnham log cabin in Josephine County in 1908. The roof and shelving are made of split cedar. The shelves are lined with provisions, coffee featuring prominently. The United States was to become the world's major consumer of coffee.

of the stove that heated saucepans on top and the oven below. Circles were cut out of the cast iron on top of the stove to allow the flame to come into direct contact with the saucepan. Plates over these circles covered the flame when the stove was not in use. There was a warming oven above the flat surface and a griddle area to the side for making griddle cakes. Usually the fire was started with kindling wood and the stove was heated quickly before coals were added. Most experienced housekeepers would bank the coals before going to bed at night to keep the fire-box warm, the flue drawing, and the room at least a little warm. The wood stove was the perfect spot to read by.

Wood was also used as a building material. Norwegian boatwrights were recruited to Seattle in the early 1900s and the natural wood that predominates in regional kitchens is a tribute to their skills. A generation or two of homeowners in the 1950s and 1960s who stripped off the intervening apple green, sunshine yellow, and robin's-egg blue paints of 1930s kitchens uncovered the first growth, straight-grained fir that was so much used in the early 1900s. Walls were tongue and groove; floors, counters, cupboards, window frames were all of wood.

Perhaps it is the Scandinavian tradition that has left Seattle with its fascination for blue and white in kitchens. I know from my experience of running a kitchen store for the last twenty years that almost anything in blue and white sells well ahead of any other colors. Perhaps, too, the preference is a vestige of that first Trading Post whose blue and white trade china was a company hallmark.

Within thirty years of the arrival of the first settlers, franchises had been written for a gas company and an electric company, both of which were formed to provide the lighting that would replace the candles and fish-oil street lamps then in use. Gas, manufactured from burning coal and bunker fuel, was first into production but electricity soon had the lighting business. At first, however, very little of either was considered for household use.

The 1930s formed the next significant growth ring when Seattle's kitchens underwent a facelift that carried them into the early 1940s without any further remodeling. Seattle City Light, a division of city government, completed massive dams and generating units in the Cascade Mountains just to the east, and set the lowest electrical rates in the country. It then offered a free electric stove to all householders who were prepared to give up their coal- and wood-burning ranges.

Many people were sentimental about their cast-iron stoves; after all, they had comforted generations of damp families, sometimes providing the primary heat source in a small house. Moreover they lasted forever— little could go wrong other than the occasional bird's nest in the chimney and its resulting smoke storm. They were also very hard to move. City Light's ploy, then, was to remove the old stoves, many of which had to be cut apart before they could be taken out of the house, in order to install the new electric stove free of charge.

C.W. Wagstaff (above) *standing by his gas stove, which he subsequently foresook in favor of the new electric range he won in the early 1930s in a jingle contest run by General Electric.*

Modernity plus. General Electric's sparkling "Better Maid" model kitchen on show at Edwards Furniture Company, Portland, in 1935 (below).

The 1930s saw the introduction of the streamlined kitchen—a super-efficient workplace (preceding pages and opposite). Ceiling fans coped with the heat, laminated surfaces were easy to keep clean, and a battery of fitted cupboards, drawers, and other storage spaces accommodated the ever-increasing clutter of appliances that were now deemed essential labor-saving devices.

These three-burner stoves featured elevated ovens—so that the housewife would not get "the bends" when baking bread—and were perched on high, spindly legs, which made the job of cleaning under the stove easier. That the old stoves sat directly on the floor and could not be cleaned underneath by anyone, escaped the attention of most modern women, who were learning to manage their homes without domestic help. Factory jobs had lured most of the helpers away from families and the housewife found herself suddenly in the position of maintaining a house, nurturing her family, and doing all the cooking as well.

This corresponded historically with both the rise of domestic science and the national movement to transfer standards from the factory to the housewife's workplace. Standards of cleanliness and efficiency as rigid as those in factories called for covering porous wood with seamless, germ-resistant linoleum. Wall surfaces had to be washable, and kitchen shelves and work spaces were now made of enamel, tile, or porcelain. Because the housewife did not want to work in drab surroundings, various colors came in and out of vogue. "Glaring white" was deemed bad on the eyes, so soothing colors like pale green or tan were recommended. Later cheerful colors became fashionable.

Built-in cupboards came into fashion for all new houses in the 1930s. As counter heights were standardized, freestanding sinks and work tables were discarded and fitted into cupboard installations. The breakfast nook was exceedingly popular in the 1930s and 1940s. The fitted cupboards made more space available and a gate-leg table with a few wooden chairs were popular additions. In grander or older houses, the butler's pantry was often converted to eating space.

In many cases, the installation of the new stove and, maybe, a new refrigerator (not supplied free, but on view at the City Light showroom and sales office) took care of kitchens until the next growth ring was formed in the postwar prosperity of the 1950s. Then the flood of new toasters, mixers, and percolators strained the electrical service and counter space of the 1930s kitchen and families were presented with the choice of either remodeling or moving to a new tract house development. Many chose the new home for its modern kitchen and new appliances. These mass-produced tract houses brought an end to much of the individuality of local kitchen design.

Residents of the Pacific northwest have weathered economic depressions with much more ease than those living in harsher climates. As a result, much of the culinary tradition revolves around the sharing of food in communal feasts. The mildly acrid aroma of salmon grilling on a barbecue outside, the scent of herbs in pots on the deck, the smell of baking, and the hint of a fruit dessert are the likely aromas in the air of a modern Seattle kitchen. Granite and marble surfaces, restaurant stove and refrigerators are its visible hallmarks. However, the kitchen is now, as it always was, the center and heartbeat of the house. All gather in its warmth, its air of sociability and soothing aromas.

CANADA
The Seasonal Kitchen

❖

A NITA S TEWART

There have been many kitchens in my life: my grand-mother's, my mother's, my friends', my own. We Canadians were, until just a generation or so ago, concerned with survival rather than culinary niceties. Our food was, and to a large extent still is, honest, hearty and, especially in rural Canada, homemade. Although most Canadians now live in urban centers, it is the rural kitchen that I am most familiar with, rather than the kitchens in the cities, which could be anywhere in the industrialized Western world.

One basic truth weaves the kitchens of Canada closely together. We are a seasonal people: our climate has dictated that. Pity the poor settlers who landed in the Maritimes or on the fringes of Upper and Lower Canadian wilderness during the summer and had to face that most Canadianizing season of all: winter. No one could have prepared them for the snow and ice, the isolation, and the lack of food. It's around this terrifying season that our food ways have developed.

Let's begin two generations ago in my grandmother's home. She grew up, married, and raised her family on a succession of farms in south central Ontario. Her kitchen was truly the heart of the home, warm and inviting—mainly because she was there. The solid ash table, a wedding gift from the Loyal Orange Lodge, was always the center of the room. On it, the children did their homework by lamplight, pigs were cut up for salting, and the traveling doctor performed tonsillectomies. A food grinder was attached so firmly to one end of the tabletop, for grinding cucumbers for relish and meat for sausage, that the old table still has the marks. Grandma did all her dressmaking on it, from work shirts to coats, and when biscuits were needed, she'd wipe off one end, pile on the flour and make the lightest scones. The old table, so full of family memories, is now in my dining room.

There were no built-in cupboards in these old kitchens. Storage space

An apple peeler (above) helped save a little time in the preparation of pies and apple sauce. Large quantities of apples were given over to cider and vinegar production.

A batch of bread is left to rise (opposite) while its intended accompaniment—butter—is in the jar alongside.

148

A store-cupboard of jams, preserves, and sauces indicates that waste is anathema to people on the land. Any surplus produce must be utilized to see out the winter.

was provided by the pantry, the pie cupboard, and the cellar. Sweet things were stored in the pie cupboard, secure from the mice that roamed in the pantry, a small room beside the kitchen. The pie cupboard had doors with fine screen or cloth panels so that air could circulate. You went down to the cellar, or "down cellar," via a stairway, although older homes simply had a hatchway in the floor of the kitchen.

The cellar had a cement or hard earth floor. There were bins in the colder part, which was often walled off from the rest. This was known as the "root cellar" after the vegetables that were stored there. Preserves, jams, and pickles were also stored on shelves in the cool, dark cellar.

The floor of the kitchen was usually patterned linoleum laid over wooden, often pine, planks. The walls were painted and sometimes decorated with wallpaper. Coal oil lamps provided the lighting.

All meals were eaten in the kitchen. Breakfast was large and hearty. There would be eggs, boiled in a solid aluminum pot or fried in a cast-iron skillet, porridge made from oats that were ground and toasted locally, and a slice of homemade bread soaked in boiling water before being doused with cream and brown or maple sugar. At harvest time or a barn raising, when there were extra men at the table, potatoes and meats were added. Toast was made by placing bread in a wire holder and setting it over the coals on the wood stove. Sometimes coffee was served, but tea was undoubtedly the preferred beverage.

The unpasteurized cream for the porridge came from "down cellar," where it was kept cool in a cream can with a tight-fitting lid. It had been separated in the barn where milk was saved for feeding the pigs. Extra cream was allowed to sour, then sent to the dairy to be made into butter. Cheese was usually purchased, although some families, usually Mennonite, made Easter cheese in the spring.

Grandma did all her baking on a wood-fired stove but gave herself over completely to the joys of an electric range in the 1940s. She never did quite master the intricacies of lighting a gas oven and once nearly blew us all to Kingdom Come. She baked bread daily with yeast or "mother" that was saved from year to year in a crock in the cellar. This original sourdough was passed from one farm family to another. It was a matter of status whose was older and better.

Grandma served the largest meal at noon when the men came in from the fields ravenously hungry. She would boil potatoes—enough to fry leftovers for supper—and serve these with a roast of meat or fried pork chops, a boat full of gravy, perhaps some home-canned peas, beans, or stewed tomatoes, a glass dish brimming with pickled beets or governor's sauce (a green tomato pickle that exemplifies how short our summers are), "boughten" bread when they had extra money, some homemade tin biscuits, jam, butter, honey, a fruit pie or two, and a fat brown Betty pot of tea. In the summer, she picked lettuce from the garden and poured on a cream and vinegar dressing. Fresh cucumbers floated in sweetened vinegar, sometimes with a sprinkling of chopped green onion.

Supper was also a large meal because the men had chores to do in the

Easter cheese strains in an old blue granite-ware colander (above). *This special dessert, made just once a year, is served with first-run maple syrup. Behind stands a panful of butter tarts. The older the pan, the better it is for baking.*

A gargantuan stove (left) *is surrounded by equally handsome kitchen utensils.*

barn afterwards. It was often potatoes fried in dripping or butter, perhaps a plate of sliced cold beef or pork, more pies, and a cake. Each diner had a "nappie" (a shallow dish) of preserved fruit which was eaten with either hot biscuits or homemade bread and butter. It was, as I remember, very sweet and delicious.

The preparation of such meals required a tremendous amount of work, both inside the home and outside. The harvesting year began, as it still does, in late February when the winter days begin to lengthen and warm. The sap starts to run and fills the branches of the sugar maple trees with spring strength. Holes are drilled through the tree bark about 4 feet (1.2 meters) above the level of the snow, spigots are banged into place, and a bucket is hung on a little hook to catch the sweet, watery sap. It is then boiled, either in large iron sugar kettles or in huge flat pans placed over a wood fire. Forty gallons (180 liters) of sap yield one gallon (4.5 liters) of sweet maple syrup.

Maple syrup and maple sugar are made from the sap of the rock or sugar maple and the black maple, which grow in southeastern Canada. The methods of harvesting and boiling down the sap were taught to the early colonists by the Indians. Once the syrup is made, a further reduction by a quarter will produce maple sugar. In colonial days this was used as a sweetener and often represented part-payment of wages. Here (above) the sap is poured into casks and (below) evaporated in large pans over a wood fire. People who like candy can still employ the traditional method of making it: boil some maple syrup until it reaches the soft-ball stage, then pour it onto a patch of thick snow. The syrup will harden to a chewy consistency.

The garden played the most important role in feeding the family, and all the surplus produce was preserved for the bleak winter. My grandparents canned the peas, tomatoes, and some of the beans; pickled the beets in a spicy marinade; dilled the beans and cucumbers; ground up other yellow-ripe cucumbers into relish; boiled the ripe tomatoes with sugar and spices into chili sauce; preserved the currants and berries in sugar syrup or simmered them into jam. The cabbage was salted, then fermented into sauerkraut. The papery-skinned onions were tied into ropes and hung from the cellar rafter. Wild fruits—elderberries, chokecherries, and grapes—were picked along the hedgerows to make sparkling jellies or deep rich pies.

Carrots, potatoes, turnips, a few heads of winter cabbage, and squash were stored in the root cellar through the long winter months with little spoilage. The potato sprouts were trimmed off in the spring and the small spuds were kept for seed.

Every farm had an orchard, in which were all the old-fashioned varieties of apples, several pear trees, a plum tree or two, and a cherry tree that invariably fed more birds than people. In the autumn apples were, and still are, a major harvest. Beginning about the first of August when the Yellow Transparents were ready, apple sauce was made and put through a cone-shaped sieve before being canned. As the season progressed, apples were sliced and diced by a group of women who got together and had a "bee." They would do bushels. Other apples were pressed for cider, but since my grandparents were abstainers, they drank their apple juice immediately or made it into apple cider vinegar; other farm families let it become "hard" and quite alcoholic. Some of the apples were taken to the cider mill to be pressed and cooked into apple butter—a smooth, deliciously sweet, dark brown spread. Smeared on fresh warm biscuits, it made a quick tea snack or after-supper treat. The rest of the bountiful apple harvest was stored in the cellar along with a bushel of late-ripening pears.

Hearty meals and large groups made for a lot of washing-up. Powerful alkaline lye soap cleaned the dishes, but left its mark on the hands of those on washing-up duty.

In August, the oats, barley, wheat, and buckwheat were threshed. The grain was used mainly for animal feed, though the buckwheat blossoms did provide dark and pungent honey. Using a system called "trading hands," the men of the neighborhood participated in each other's harvest. Each family in turn provided the food. The men breakfasted at their own homes, then went to the fields.

The baking had begun the day before. A dozen or so loaves of white bread, at least twelve pies, a few batches of biscuits, and five or six cakes were all made in Grandma's kitchen. Any perishable pies, such as coconut cream or lemon meringue, were stored on a swing shelf suspended from the ceiling by wires in the cellar. Some families did have ice-boxes in the kitchen but most of the ice that was cut on the local lake in January and February was stored in sawdust-filled sheds and sold to ice-cream merchants in the nearby town. The rest of the baking went into the pantry or the pie cupboard. All the cutlery, dishes, baking supplies—even the coal lamps—were also stored in either of those two locations.

Beef or pork roasts were cooked slowly in the wood stove throughout the morning. Pickles were brought up from storage, lettuce and green onions picked, and new potatoes boiled. Extra boards were added to the great old table until its length almost filled the kitchen. It was draped with a white tablecloth, set with Grandma's special china, and loaded with food. After the workers left, the dishes were cleared, hot water was taken from the reservoir at the end of the cook stove, and the dishes were washed with her skin-sizzling lye soap. Then it all began again in preparation for the next meal.

Each farm kept animals for food. Chickens, geese, and ducks ran at will throughout the barnyard and the fenced meadow. Chicken eggs were

Blue and red enliven the otherwise rustic tones of this timber kitchen.

eaten, but the duck eggs were not. The fertilized goose eggs were nurtured in a pail of oats in the pantry until the mother goose was ready to sit on her nest. Roast goose was *the* meat of celebration, so it was very important to coax a large flock of goslings into existence.

In the autumn or early winter a pig was killed and scalded in boiling water in the sugar kettle, so that the hair could be scraped off more easily. The meat was cut up with heavy butcher's knives, salted, and stored in a pork barrel in the dirt-floored basement. The fat was heated slowly until it melted, poured into containers, and left to harden until needed for baking. It was also made into soap using lye that was purchased at the local general store. The lye and fat were cooked together slowly on an open bonfire in the sugar kettle, then shaped into huge, soft slabs which were sliced into usable chunks.

Most of the pork was cooked, packed into glass sealers, covered with rendered fat and sealed before storing in the cold room. Sausages, too, were made in the kitchen: they were sometimes smoked, sometimes used fresh, and sometimes canned, again covered in fat.

Gathering and preparing food was thus a full-time occupation for my grandmother and her peers. My farming friends follow much the same regimen as my grandparents, except that the size of their landholding under intensive cultivation sometimes reaches thousands of acres. The farm wife usually works at a second or even third job to make ends meet: many are university-educated professionals.

The old woodstove has given way to a self-cleaning oven, the pantry and the cool, dusty cellar have been replaced by a frost-free refrigerator and at least one freezer. The dishes are done with environmentally friendly soap in a state-of-the-art dishwasher. The basic tenet, however, is the same as a century ago: inordinately hard work, long hours, seven days a week.

Canadians still obey the seasons, but it is no longer a life-threatening situation when we do not get around to canning the tomatoes or milling the flour. Gardens are still important and farmers' markets abound. Brimming with every conceivable type of produce, they provide a way for urbanites to savor the land from which most of them came.

Elements of rusticity in the log cabin still have their place in more modern surroundings. The appeal of patterned plates, gleaming copperware, and family mementoes never fades. However, few people have difficulty embracing the efficiencies of the modern age, no matter how romantic old-fashioned methods may seem.

The First Kitchen
Whittier, California

❖

M. F. K. Fisher

It is impossible for me to think of the first kitchen in my memory without connecting it with my Grandfather Holbrook. This is odd because I don't remember him at all, although I think I met him once just before his death. I must have been very young, since I was almost four when Grandmother Holbrook, his widow, came to live with us.

Elements from the homespun kitchens of the nineteenth century have been upheld as desirable design features in the "country-style" kitchens of the late twentieth century (above and opposite). Stainless steel sinks and efficient fuel systems have taken the hard work out of rusticity.

The first kitchen was in the big house in Whittier where we lived from my third year until I was almost twelve, and I clearly remember thinking that it was the nastiest room I had ever seen in my life, and wondering how my mother and father could stand to have good things come from it. They ate very well from there always, and I myself learned to cook in its dark green, shadowy depths.

The kitchen was long, narrow, and dank, and it was the ugliest room in the house. It was lit by one electric bulb hanging from the center of the ceiling directly above the kitchen table, with its two bins for flour and sugar underneath, and its chipped white enamel top. The only natural light came from two high windows above the kitchen sink at one end of the room, which I never was tall enough to look out of. There was probably a view of the house next door, but I don't remember ever seeing anything except a patch of sky far above the old sink.

The sink had a counter on either side and it was very ugly, like everything else in the room. The gas stove was against the far wall from the door into the dining room. There were many cupboards and one cooler and, of course, a small icebox. There was linoleum on the floor. Between the dining room and the kitchen there was a small mysterious sliding door which was supposed to open onto a built-in sideboard in the dining room, but it was never used. The cook-of-the-moment brought everything in through the swinging door.

Mother had an electric bell under her foot that summoned the help from the kitchen, but she could seldom find it and instead would ring a little silver bell. Father sat at the kitchen end of the table and Mother at

the far end so that she could keep one eye on the swinging door. I never knew how it was managed so smoothly, but the service was always good. We children never addressed the hired help during a meal, nor she any of us, although we might have been jabbering happily to each other just before entering the dining room.

At the sink and window end of the kitchen, which was painted greenish brown, a door led onto the porch, also long and narrow, with a small toilet and a tiny stuffy room, with one window at its end for the current slavey. The room was without ornament of any kind, and, I suppose, contained the usual bed and chair and even a bureau. The woman who occupied it was supposed to use the back toilet and do all her other personal functions in the kitchen sink. She was off every Thursday evening and Sunday after lunch, and was considered part of the family, but always in a subservient way.

It seems odd now that I was raised with a strange woman always in the house, an imposition I never did like. My mother, who was born and raised on the plains of Iowa, considered such services as part of her life and always had someone to help with the daily chores, or, in fact, to perform all of them. Most of her hired help had been Swedish and Norwegian immigrants learning the language, but in California she had to accustom herself to live with a much more motley group of people.

Our first maid-of-all-work was a very large fat black woman named Cynthia, who was without any pretensions or prejudices. She was there the first winter we were in Whittier and had the bedroom next to the bathroom upstairs. When Grandmother Holbrook came to live with us, the servant's room was added onto the back of the house along with a little apartment for the autocratic old Irish lady.

Cynthia was wonderful, with warm skin, and my little sister Anne and I loved to crawl into bed with her and softly sing hymns and pray to her God. She sat proudly in the middle of the back seat of the Model-T Ford on Sundays, when we went for our weekly drive, with Anne and me on either side of her, and with Mother and Father sitting grandly in the front seat, dressed in their dusters and Mother in a veil and driving hat. Cynthia seemed much grander, and we were especially admired by anyone who saw the spectacle when she wore a high turban of blue satin with a matching dress which she inherited from Mother. It was cut very low with insets of brown lace which did not show at all on her skin, so that she looked like a half-naked goddess.

Cynthia soon left because she was the only black woman in Whittier, and when she went to the grocery store for Mother, nobody spoke to her: nobody had seen her at all. "I am invisible here," she said, "I must go."

Mother and Anne and I wept, and even Father was much moved, although he admitted that he had always hated to go into the bathroom for his morning shave after Cynthia had steamed up the windows with her bath.

That was my first brush with racism, and the last bath ever taken by a servant in the house, as far as I know.

After Cynthia left, Anne and I grew to accept the fact that cooks lived downstairs in their own quarters. My father was amazed to learn early on that he and Mother were considered kind to their help. I was always puzzled by the difference between the cook's new quarters downstairs and our own bedrooms upstairs. There must have been some signs of the various occupants of that little room but I don't remember any of them, not even a picture of a relative or a book or magazine. Anne and I freely used the back toilet, which made us feel close to the cook. We would spend long hours in that stuffy little cubby-hole, taking turns sitting on the toilet and listening to my continued stories, most of which concerned imaginary characters connected with World War I.

I remember talking seriously with Mother several times about why the servant's room was so ugly but she would tell me that she and Father were the best employers, and she also boasted to me that her own father had felt that domestic help should form a union. Grandfather Holbrook proposed it several times before his death, but he was always laughed at.

The work of craftsmen and artisans was gradually replaced by house fittings and appliances made in bulk in factories. In the mid-nineteenth century, designer Catharine Beecher (sister of the author of Uncle Tom's Cabin) *began to advocate the kitchen as "workroom"—a compact unit as efficient and as economical in its use of space as a ship's galley, but pleasant to work in nonetheless. The kitchen she designed for her sister over one hundred years ago was the forerunner of the sleek, gleaming, modern American kitchen we know today, like the kitchen pictured above.*

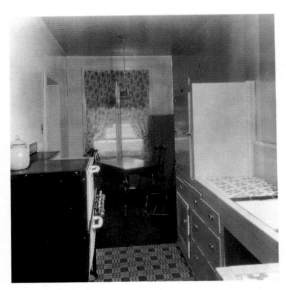

The breakfast nook retained some of the warmth of yesteryear that had been lost with the adoption of streamlined cookers and glittering surfaces.

The kitchen remained dank and unappetizing, although it was most enjoyable when Mother would go down to make an annual cake for my father's birthday. (It was a Lady Baltimore, for some reason.) And there were times when Grandmother would supervise the making of jam there in the dark room, when once a year several cousins would appear bringing fruit from their ranches, and the kitchen would be full of laughter and good smells from the pots. Mostly, though, it was a place to be avoided by everybody but me, except on Sunday nights when we had to make our own supper . . . very simple things like oyster stew or scrambled eggs.

I soon learned that the best way to get attention was to cook something, and I easily fell into the role of the cook's helper. I loved to stand on a little stool and stir things carefully in a double-boiler, so that I soon became known as the family cook on the regular cook's night out. From early on I was helping her make cake on Saturday morning for Sunday noon.

After Cynthia, the best girls we ever had in the kitchen were four middle-aged sisters called the McClure girls. They lived with their father far down on Painter Avenue and we never knew which of them would be serving breakfast. Bertha was tall and thin and very nervous, so that when she served coffee or tea the cups rattled in their saucers. We were aware that Bertha had a crush on Father and watched eagerly as she slid around his unconscious head and tittered helplessly when he addressed her directly.

Our favorite of the four sisters was Margaret. She was almost as small as we were . . . a tiny woman with a cleft palate. Anne and I used to pray with her often in her bedroom, and were unaware that for a long time we were speaking just as she spoke, as if we had cleft palates too. Grandmother and Mother finally forbade Margaret to come to the house at all, as we always spoke as she did when she was anywhere near us. This became, in fact, a kind of fetish with my parents, especially my mother, and we had a hard time breaking ourselves of this habit. Margaret-Talk became our secret language, and finally we had only to mutter the words "sixty-four" in her strange cleft palate accent to feel safe and loving, two united against the world. This continued until my sister died when I was fifty-seven and she was fifty-five, but it was a secret between us.

Margaret was the last of the four sisters to come, and I think I began to use the kitchen more as a show-off place after she left. By the time I was ten, I was thoroughly familiar with cooking in that dreadful room. I knew its worst secrets and knew equally well that there was no use in protesting its many discomforts. By then I could bake a fairly decent sponge cake and learned not to experiment with changing the proportions of spices and such in recipes. I no longer needed to stand on a little stool to stir the white sauces and less commendable messes, which catered to my Grandmother's austere ideas of correct eating.

We left for the country when we moved down Painter Avenue across the county road and onto Painter Extension. The kitchen there was bright and cheerful and the servant's quarters were separate from the

Linoleum, enamel, and glazed ceramic were the wonder surfaces of the 1930s. They were easy to keep clean, a boon to the housewife who had to rely increasingly on her own skills rather than those of a domestic help.

house. By then, I realized that Mother and Father were indeed good employers, but I always wondered how they could have subjected other human beings to such sordid conditions as were taken for granted in the first big house on Painter.

I wished fervently that I had known my Grandfather, and I still do, because he sowed the seeds in me of protest against conditions that were considered normal. He probably would have enjoyed the same good food and he might never have voiced his critical views to other people most connected with these same views. He was most certainly not an agitator, anymore than they were eager to be disturbed. In other words, it would all have continued in the usual patterns, but it is a comfort to know that my grandfather felt strongly about the conditions of servants in America. And I don't think that by now there are any slaveys, as we took for granted. Neither Grandfather nor I did anything to change the situation, but I feel sure that Cynthia would no longer be invisible even in Whittier, and that anyone who had to live in that little room off the back porch would see to it that a bathroom was available somewhere in the house. Grandfather would still be a stranger to me, and I would still make white sauces for Grandmother, and practice the powers that lurked behind my continued interest in cooking. In other words, the more things change, the more they are the same.

PERU
A Merging of Cultures

❖

ELISABETH LAMBERT ORTIZ

At its height in the early sixteenth century, the Inca Empire stretched from what is now Ecuador, to Peru, Bolivia, part of Chile, and into the northwest corner of Argentina. Between the desert of South America's west coast and the rainforests of the Amazon, a great civilization flourished in the valleys and plateaux of the Andes mountains with their permanently snow-covered peaks.

Brilliant agriculturalists, the Incas were the first cultivators of the potato, the sweet potato, various kinds of corn including popcorn, many types of chili pepper—called *ají* in Quechua, the local language—and peanuts. They terraced the difficult land and built a chain of great stone cities linked by a highway on which llamas were used as pack animals. Foods from the outlying farms were brought into the cities to central markets of a type still found throughout Latin America.

On the desert coast of the west, there were small oases where the fifty or so rivers—more streams or brooks than rivers, really—came down from the Andes. The pre-Columbian peoples used this irrigation to create prosperous societies ruled by the highland Inca, a god-king. They cultivated corn, lima beans, some root crops and fruit, and they harvested fish and shellfish from the sea. From the highlands they obtained freeze-dried potatoes. This process took advantage of the freezing nights of the Andean mountains. Potatoes were spread out overnight to freeze. When they thawed in the morning sun the women trampled out the water. After about three of these freezings and thawings, all the water had been extracted from the potatoes and they would keep indefinitely.

This coastal civilization was swept away by the Spanish conquest but in time a new, Spanish-dominated society evolved, with the nation's capital, Lima, on the coast. Those highland Indians who survived worked as serfs on the great Spanish haciendas but in the more inaccessible valleys the original inhabitants were undisturbed and continued to pursue their own way of life.

This illustration (above) dates from 1620 and depicts the harvesting of potatoes in June, an important part of the traditional Peruvian agricultural cycle.

A woman peels a potato (opposite). Potatoes still play an important part in the Peruvian diet.

A woman prepares anticuchos and potatoes on a makeshift barbecue. Potatoes are also prepared in rather more elaborate ways in Peruvian cooking such as with cream cheese, onions, and orange juice. They are also mashed with shrimps and hard-cooked eggs and used in the thick stews (chupes) to which milk has been added to make them more liquid than their Chilean counterparts.

In the centuries following the birth of agriculture in the Valley of Mexico in about 7000 BC, the foods grown there had spread all over the Caribbean, Central and South America, where they mingled with the indigenous foods. It was already a lavish larder, but when joined by the foods brought by the Spanish conquerors, farmers and cooks had an even wider choice. Out of this meeting of worlds came colonial Peruvian cooking, still resting firmly on its Inca foundations but absorbing and adapting to the new influences.

At the time of the conquest, Spain had only just liberated itself from its Islamic conquerors, so there was also a considerable Arab influence in the colonial kitchen, not least in the beautiful tiles used to decorate the walls. These were mostly green and golden yellow, imported from Seville where they are still made today. Kitchens were large, dictated by the feudal patterns of society introduced by the Spanish to replace the Inca welfare state, about whose kitchens we know very little. Apart from the richly decorated tiles, the early coastal people had colorful woven textiles and magnificent pottery. There was a charcoal-burning stove on which to cook and earthenware casseroles to contain the food.

Nowadays, except in very remote mountain villages, lighting is by electricity. In earlier times there might have been candles, though more probably kitchens would have been lit by kerosene or gas lamps. There would be a table and chairs, shelves and cupboards for storage. Cooking was done by the servants, who ate in the kitchen. The family ate in the dining room.

The kitchens were bright with heaps of small, hot green peppers; large, thick-fleshed, bright red rocotos (very hot peppers); smaller, tapering yellow and orange mirasols (a slightly less hot pepper); bright red, ripe tomatoes; green herbs; strings of small dried red peppers; yellow and deep purple corn, and fruits from both the temperate zones (apricots) and the tropics (bananas and pineapples).

Cooking in the colonial kitchen was a mixture of Quechua Indian and Spanish, which combined local produce and introduced foods in the cookpot. *Ají de Gallina* is an example of such a marriage. It translates roughly as "Hot Chili Pepper of Hen," though a less literal translation, "Chicken in Pepper Sauce," more accurately describes it. The dish combines vegetable oil, milk, walnuts, and cheese from the Old World with tomatoes and peppers from the New. Onions and garlic are sautéed as in European cooking; the tomatoes and peppers are reduced to a purée in a traditional stone mortar, called a *batan* in Peru. After slow poaching on the charcoal stove, the chicken is skinned, boned, and shredded, then added to a tomato–chili walnut sauce to heat through. This is a typical Quechua cooking method, though the ground walnuts that thicken the sauce are a contribution from the Middle East via Spain.

The potato inevitably played a large role in colonial cooking: there were innumerable varieties in a multiplicity of sizes, shapes, and colors. One of the most popular, still available, was a large, yellow-fleshed potato used in the traditional dish *Ocopa Arequipeña*, in which boiled, peeled,

and halved potatoes were arranged cut-side down on a bed of lettuce, then masked with a thick cheese, hot pepper, and walnut sauce. It would almost certainly be served on a large and attractive ceramic platter, and garnished with halved hard-boiled eggs cut-side up, all white and gold, perhaps designed to honor the sun god and moon goddess worshipped by the Inca people.

The charcoal stove was ideal for the highland kitchen where, because of the altitude, liquids boil at a lower temperature and therefore the cooking of soups and stews is necessarily slow and gentle. It also adapted easily to grilling, especially for that most Peruvian of all appetizers: *anticuchos*, for which small pieces of beef heart, marinated in seasoned vinegar, are threaded on skewers, grilled, and served with a very hot chili and annatto sauce. Annatto, or *achiote*, is an orange-yellow coloring made from the seeds of a tropical flowering tree.

The traditional highland methods of long, slow cooking were also popular in sea-level kitchens, where cooks used very, very low heat to achieve the same result. Despite the great differences in altitude, many dishes were held in common. The rich harvest from the sea—the gift of the cold Humboldt Current—which includes scallops and corvina (striped bass), is cooked with equal relish by the cook in the mountains

A rural family surrounded by cooking pots and clothing. The traditional woven fabrics are characterized by the use of solid masses of color in stripes or in small squares of contrasting hue.

and the cook at sea level. *Ceviche*, raw fish marinated in lime juice, requires only a good lemon squeezer, which the superb potters of the Inca civilization created a long time ago.

A further advantage of the charcoal stove was that it was admirably suited to the making of stocks, much used in all Latin American cooking, and soups. Soup is still a great favorite and is served at all main meals. On the coast Peruvian fish soups, called *chupes*, are traditional. They use mostly local ingredients, especially annatto and fresh lima beans, which, as their name implies, were first cultivated in Peru. It is believed that soup was made in Peru long before cookpots were invented, probably as far back as neolithic times. Red-hot stones, heated in the fire, were put into wood, hollowed out to form a rough bowl, and filled with water and any available meat, herbs, or vegetables. The hot stones boiled the water and the result was an early form of soup or stew.

Not quite as old as the hollowed-out log but still one of the earliest forms of cooking is the *pachamanca*, a Quechua word meaning "earth oven." Here the cook's room has the sky for its ceiling and all outdoors for its walls. It is a primitive form of cooking which has survived from early empires through the Spanish conquest and the colonial kitchen to the present day; its geographical span stretches from New England in the north of North America, to Chile in the south of South America. What started as an ingenious necessity has become festival food, marking holidays and joyous occasions with family, friends, and neighbors gathered to enjoy the feast in the open air.

Small rolls made from maize flour. Maize crops produce a heavy yield but the cereal lacks the gluten necessary to make leavened bread and is a relatively poor source of nourishment.

Adobe-brick house and outdoor clay oven with a domed top.

When the Pilgrims landed from England in Massachusetts, they encountered the local Indians enjoying what is now called a clambake. In Chile the clambake, in which the food is covered with seaweed and cooked in a pit with hot stones, can be a very lavish affair called a *curanto*. It takes advantage of Chile's magnificent seafood and can include lobsters, oysters, mussels, scallops, and crabs, as well as vegetables such as peas, beans, and potatoes, and meat such as sausages and a whole suckling pig.

Peru's *pachamanca*, the Quechua variety of the earth oven, is very grand indeed. After the pit has been dug, the wood burned down and the stones heated, the pit is lined with moist green leaves and aromatic herbs. On top of this are placed a suckling pig or baby goat, guinea pigs or chickens. Casseroles with rice are topped with corn, potatoes, sweet potatoes, tamales, in fact, whatever tradition, imagination, and income dictate. More green leaves go on top before the pit is sealed with hot stones and a thick layer of earth to allow the contents to cook. While the food is cooking, the pit might be decorated with green branches, or even perhaps flowers.

Though in the past all this cooking was done outdoors, the cook of the colonial kitchen took advantage of a well-equipped indoor room with a table, knives, and stove to make sauces and salads, which were then served in marvelous pottery bowls. The colonial cook's legacy is still being enjoyed by modern cooks, with only the addition of a blender or food processor to provide a twentieth-century contribution to the scene.

Freezing and drying the potato crop ensures supplies over an extended period of time. The potatoes have to be soaked in order to reconstitute them for cooking.

MIDDLE EAST & NORTH AFRICA

❖

Morocco   A Kitchen in Sille

MOROCCO
A Traditional *Dweeria*

❖

JILL TILSLEY-BENHAM

Subtly spiced chicken (top) *features in dishes such as* couscous *and* tajines.

Kebabs (above) *originated in Turkey.*

A large cooking vessel stands above a charcoal-filled metal naffekh (opposite).

The city of Fez, when I was young, a house in the medina. A drowsy, ancient, perfumed house, haunted by mischievous jnoun. At its heart a courtyard, shadowed by sweet-lemon trees, paved with marble and mosaic. A fountain, bird song, jasmine, peace. Shades of the Alhambra.

The courtyard doors are keyhole shaped, patterned with arabesques. One leads to a chamber for dining, another to the cook's domain, the *dweeria*, or "little house." A misnomer this "little" for it caters for thirty or so: a family spanning four generations. A genteel family, well-to-do, with servants in plenty to feed.

It is dark in that lofty kitchen, depressingly dark, but to let in the sun is to let in heat. Three golden shafts, no more, pierce the slits let high in one wall—less windows than smell-extractors. For serious light, one must open either the scullery door (which leads straight onto a narrow street) or the courtyard door of the kitchen itself.

Forming the shape of an L (with a Moorish arch at its joint), kitchen and scullery are big rooms both. Whitewashed twice a year, for charcoal is a dirty fuel, the high stone walls are massively thick; a further precaution against summer's heat.

A sense of space, for there is no cosy clutter, no furnishings other than two or three *midat*—round wooden tables, less than knee-high, surrounded by cushions or squat little stools. One table appears to be wearing a hat, a pointed hat like that of a witch. Woven from pale esparto grass, brightly patterned, morocco trimmed, it is now guarding Cook's *kebabs*; keeping off flies, keeping in heat. An unsolved puzzle, as yet, is how this dual-purpose container also keeps bread and pastries so fresh. Could it be the conical shape? The "pyramid factor" as some suggest? Whatever the reason, the *t'baq* does a fine job, be it woven from grass, or doum-palm leaves, or splendidly wrought from silvered copper. And it's no less efficient at keeping food hot—an important factor in Morocco, where the myriad courses of a *diffa*, or feast, are left to wait at the dining hall door.

Three traditional Moroccan utensils.
A simple earthenware naffekh *(top). Earthenware painted with brilliant blue, brown, and green emblems spread from Baghdad around AD 800 to reach Egypt, Morocco, and Andalusia. The use of vibrant color in conjunction with an appreciation of the matt simplicity of earthenware prevails today.* Tajine slaoui *(center), a glazed earthenware dish for slow-cooked dishes such as the* tajine *of mutton with quinces and honey.* Midouna, *a woven platter (above).*

Copper pans and skillets hang from the walls, their sand-and-lemon scoured brilliance relieving the gloom somewhat. Larger vessels, such as the *gsaa*, spend much of their day on the red-tiled floor, their night in the scullery *s'klebia*, a roomy walk-in larder. A shallow bowl of wood or clay, the *gsaa* is used for making doughs and tiny pellets of *couscous*. Steamed in a *couscoussier* (often above a companion stew), this fine but filling Berber food early became the national dish.

There are no more cupboards, only shelves, and on these range graded *tajine slaoui*, the shallow, conical-lidded pot in which *tajine* (another type of Moorish stew) is left for hours to simmer. Here, too, are the small clay jars for water (fumed before use with mastic resin), and the everyday bowls and plates. Glazed, unglazed, warm brown, ochre . . . those blues and greens unique to Fez, produced from local minerals. Many are plain, but some are patterned with coal-black tar, others with glowing polychrome tints. Moorish designs (geometric, semi-floral) cover the shelves as well, for these were bought, already adorned, from craftsmen in the *Nejjarine*, the Fassi carpenter's *souk*. Also from this market came the carved wooden hammers (made for smashing sugar-cones), the lemon wood whisks and spoons, the chopping boards of olive wood, so oddly whorled and streaked. Not that these are used much, for the maids dice, with a death-sharp knife, onions flat in the palm of a hand, parsley straight into the pot—Cook, meanwhile, whipping dozens of eggs to a helpless froth with no more than her bared, black arm.

There are two types of stove, both charcoal fed. The *kanoun*, a simple tiled range with a few holes for burners, and the *naffekh* (or *mejmeh*); a round or rectangular portable brazier. Unlike the *kanoun*, whose wide funnel-shaped chimney safely draws off carbon monoxide, the *naffekh* is kept out of doors until its noxious fumes disperse. The most common sort, of plain or painted clay, is no more than a dumpy dish, but those wrought from metal, especially brass, may be tall, ornamental affairs.

The rectangular type, with its rim notched for skewers (*m'ghazel* of handsome silver, or steel), is used mainly for grilling such Moorish delights as cumin-spiced *kefta*, classic *kebabs*, and *boulfaf* of caul-wrapped liver. With its trio of pan-supporting knobs, the round *naffekh* holds skillets, kettles, mint-tea pots, the tall *couscoussier*, and earthen *tajines*. It is also used for two kinds of pastry. The first of these, the diaphanous *warka*, is formed by dabbing dough, yo-yo style, onto a hot copper tray, or *tobsil dial warka*. The result is as fine as a butterfly's wing—which cannot be said of the second sort, its venerable ancestor, *trid*. Praised by Mohammed himself (who loved only his favorite wife the more), *trid* is hand-stretched in the *gsaa*, then dried for use on a big-bellied pot, the *gdra dial trid*.

Town kitchens, unlike those in the country, seldom boast an oven, and thus evolved the method of baking known as *bin nar-ayen*, literally "between two fires." For this, the food in its pot is put on the stove, then covered with a tray, or lid, spread with glowing charcoal. Flat "tajine" loaves and joints of meat are sometimes browned this way, but the baker's

vast oven is normally used. Imprinted with a special sign for ease of identification, the daily bread, or *khobz*, is carried there by servant or child. (Housewives with neither, in this kindly town, can always seek help from a male passer-by.)

The cavernous furnace of the *hammam*, or public bath, offers a baking service too, and there can be found, stacked overnight, amphora packed with *tangia*, the comforting "bachelor's stew," and garlicky *hergma*, a robust sheep's-trotter *tajine*.

A favorite spot of the little black maids is the open scullery door. In their brilliant gowns (and out of Cook's eye), they squat, and giggle, and tend their smoking *naffekh* with bellows. Here, too, they make the most of the light, sorting out stones from lentils and wheat, pouncing on tiny bugs in the rice.

To this same door come all provisions. Sacks of fuel, being too messy to carry far, are stowed in the scullery larder, together with food enough for a week. Long-term goods are taken up to the *bit ala'oula*, a larger room on the second floor, built into a curve of the winding stairs. Packed with such basics as flour and oil, the massive "Ali Baba" jars, or *khabiat*, are then used to top up their smaller relations kept in the larder below.

Also stored in this upper room is the copper *qettara*: a still used for stealing the essence of roses. Less romantic preserves are in evidence too—salted lemons (craved by the pregnant), the jerked meat *khleii*

Cereals, stuffed vegetables, dried fruits, grilled meats, and elaborate pastries play an integral part in Moroccan cuisine (top). A tripe couscous (above) includes oil, garlic, cumin, caraway, beans, and sausage.

Some water supplies are piped. Otherwise, water must be drawn from a well.

Silverware (opposite) is an important part of the ritual of making tea. Gunpowder is one of the Chinese varieties of green tea popular throughout north Africa, particularly Morocco where it is often served flavored with mint. Green tea is unfermented, the fresh leaves being dried immediately after picking.

Elaborately crafted silverware is used in the washing of hands.

(pegged out on the roof like washing to dry), and jars of vintage *smen*, a powerful clarified butter that puts gorgonzola cheese to shame.

All Fassi houses could boast piped water by the fourteenth century. The old marble fountain, then, which graces the scullery wall, is not an unusual feature. Handsomely paneled with mosaic, this *s'kaia* provides river water for washing-up. Splashing coolly from its basin—such sweet music in summer—the overflow is carried away by a long open channel cut into the floor. This quaint, but useful, indoor stream eventually serves the house latrines.

Spring water, for drinking, comes from a brass pump-action tap fitted near the fountain's spout. This nineteenth-century addition now supplements the courtyard well—a discreet hole, lidded with marble, tucked out of the way in a corner. Had this been sunk in the kitchen instead, where beauty is not of the essence, it would have had walls and a pulley too. The fine courtyard fountain, its pool bedecked with hibiscus flowers, is only of practical use when the scullery *s'kaia* blocks: a not unusual occurrence when children play near its source—or someone upsets the *jnoun* in the drain. Loving to live near water, these impudent sprites abound in the *s'kaia*, and thus the maids go in constant fear of causing them harm or offence. An infant *jnoun* scalded with washing-up water? Then tit for tat, a child of the house will suffer the same. When the *dada* cook first arrived she burned placatory incense, and sprinkled milk, as a symbol of peace, all over the spotless floor. A pillow-plump black Shahrazad, she rivets all with her ghoulish tales—and those children who tremble within her bright skirts will *always* have care for the *jnoun* in the drain.

All upper-middle-class households depend on these negro *dadas*. Slaves at one time (though in name only), they yet command enormous respect. Fearing none but the master (and the *jnoun*), each reigns confident and supreme in her own small world, be it that of a cook, housekeeper, or nanny.

Although she was taught by her own mother's *dada*, the mistress of this house cooks only on special occasions—and then she avoids the kitchen itself, with its pounding mortars and sugar-hammers, its eerie shadows, and resident smells. No, the courtyard is this lady's kitchen, and there she sits in the sweet fresh air, with her lemon wood whisk, and her Fez-blue bowl, tending a little clay *naffekh*.

A traditional *dweeria*, yes, indeed, but how did it compare to other cooks' rooms, those in less privileged Moorish homes?

Closely, very closely, for at best it was still quite a primitive place. Size would be the main difference, and the choice and quality of utensils. There'd be few or no servants, of course, so the head of the house would do all the shopping (a daily event he greatly enjoyed), while his wife would cook with her own fair hands. But she, like her wealthy sister, tended to take her *naffekh* outside to relish that same jasmine-sweet air . . .

As for the *jnoun*, well any old water would do for them. And they weren't in the least class-conscious . . .

A Kitchen in Sille
Remnant from Turkey's Past

NEVIN HALICI

Sille is a charming town nestling between two mountains, 5 miles (8 kilometers) west of Konya in southern Anatolia, Turkey. It has been a center of settlement since before the birth of Christ and, like Konya, has outlived a succession of incursions from Hittite to Ottoman, each leaving the mark of its own civilization on the area. In the Hittite period, from about 1900 to 1200 B.C., the people of Sille lived in caves, about two hundred of which still exist. During the hegemony of the Roman Empire they were converted to Christianity.

The town of Sille (above).

Women prepare bread and pastry for a wedding (opposite). Flat bread, either with or without pockets, is made, while pastry includes the very thin yufka *(the same as* phyllo) *and* kadaif, *a shredded wheat dough.*

Sille is famous for its climate, water, vineyards, almond and walnut trees, and for the wild thyme that grows in the mountains, said to be the best in the region. The main sources of income in the area are from carpet making and pottery. While the women of Sille weave rugs with wool colored by dyes made from the nuts, the men fashion the local clay into earthenware utensils for the kitchen: pots, pitchers, casseroles, and tandir ovens. These ovens are a special feature of southern Anatolia. They are made in the pottery workshops and taken to the house to be assembled. Then they are placed in a pit dug in the earth floor of the kitchen and fueled with wood at the bottom.

Sille is isolated from the neighboring towns and villages by the surrounding mountains, and retains unique customs not even found in nearby Konya. One is the tradition that as soon as it begins to snow, a son-in-law will hurry to his mother-in-law's house to shovel the snow from her roof. The earth-covered Sille roof would leak if the snow were allowed to remain. The mother-in-law, for her part, starts to cook vermicelli pilau and halva for her son-in-law when the snow falls. She takes such care in the cooking that the men often remark wistfully, "If only it would snow, so that I can go to my mother-in-law's house to eat halva."

Most of the houses in Sille have one or two stories, though some do extend to three. Wood, stone, and earth are the building materials. *Ken*

The tandir oven originated in the Middle East and spread widely; the tandoor oven of India is a relation. Often simply a large pot set in the ground, it may also be found raised above the ground, insulated with plaster and mud.

stone, a sponge-like stone found only in Sille, ensures coolness and is used for flooring. The walls are built of stone and *kerpich* bricks made from a mixture of hay, soil, and water.

The square or rectangular kitchens are usually on the ground floor and are generally in two parts: the *bievi* or pantry where bulk supplies of food are stored, and the *asevi*, the kitchen itself, where all food is cooked; though in some smaller homes these two areas are combined. The floors of both the kitchen and the pantry are made of earth or *ken* stone and the walls are either whitewashed or glazed—the pantry walls definitely being glazed to keep the area dark. The ceilings, as in the rest of the house, are constructed with poplar-wood beams. Once, gas lamps provided light but there is electricity now. Heating comes from the cookers.

There are two types of cooker in these traditional kitchens: fixed and portable. The fixed cookers include the tandir oven, for baking bread, and an arch-shaped stone hearth built into the wall and used for roasting and frying. Both are fueled with wood. Sometimes there are two tandir ovens with a hearth in between. The portable cookers consist of two kinds of brazier: the *mangal* and the *maltiz*. The *mangal* brazier is used for cooking everyday vegetables, meat, and rice, and is fueled with oak wood, while the *maltiz* brazier burns coke to give a more intense heat for cooking sheep's heads, trotters, and tripe. The wood and coke are stored in an area near the cookers.

Cooking pots and pans are kept on a long earthen shelf, at one end of which is a bank of shelves from floor to ceiling, called *ağzi açik* (open without a door), where everyday crockery and copper pans are stored. A separate closed cupboard stores the special dinner services reserved for guests, and a second cupboard with mesh doors is used for daily leftovers and breakfast foods.

A door from the kitchen leads into the pantry, which has small windows high up in the walls to provide ventilation. Inside is a row of three grain stores in which wheat flour for baking and barley for the animals are kept for the winter. At the bottom of the wall opposite these is a step about 6 inches (15 centimeters) long and 8 inches (20 centimeters) high, usually made of stone but sometimes from a poplar tree trunk. Depressions in this step accommodate the earthenware storage jars that contain dried provisions such as sugar, bulgar (cracked wheat), vermicelli, chickpeas, lentils, beans, fruit and vegetables, as well as jams and pickles, grape molasses, fried or roasted meat, mince meat, Sille's famous salted fish, almonds, walnuts, and other titbits. The spaces between the jars are filled with onions and potatoes.

Massive jars contain essential provisions. Saucepans are either of tin-lined copper or aluminum, with pottery dishes used for oven-baked items. An alternative to the tandir is the arch-shaped hearth (above).

Cheerful textiles decorate the sitting room where meals are laid out (below). All the dishes will be served at once, often accompanied by ayran, a yogurt drink that is particularly refreshing during the hot months.

Women bake bread in an outdoor oven (opposite top). Others (below) sit beside a milk churn suspended on a wooden tripod. Butter is the common cooking agent alongside olive oil.

All these products are locally available except the fish, which is brought in, salted, and set in pots ready for the winter. It is a very popular delicacy, made only in Sille.

The third wall in the pantry—the *hevenk*—is covered with branches of the oleaster (wild olive) tree. Thick-skinned grapes are hung from these branches to keep throughout the winter. Apples, pears, and other fruit might also be hung here or kept in baskets. The fourth wall is reserved for dairy products such as cheese, yogurt, and butter, which are stored either in a cupboard or in a row of earthenware jars.

No space is wasted. Large melons and baskets filled with food hang from nails and hooks in the ceiling beams. Also hanging from the ceiling is a timber frame, called a *melak*, which is raised or lowered by ropes and used for storing *pastirma* (dried beef) and sausages. The washtub and cauldron will also be kept in the pantry, along with an assortment of other pieces of equipment, such as the dough trough, rolling pin and board, and a stone mortar for grinding the much-used thyme.

Utensils in the Sille kitchen are divided according to what they are made of: porcelain, earthenware, wood, stone, copper, iron, or glass. The dinner service and the Turkish coffee service are made from porcelain; tea, water, and sherbets are drunk from glasses. Earthenware is used for cooking pots, storage jars, pitchers (which keep water very cold), washing-up bowls, and the tandir oven. (Before piped water was available in the kitchen, washing-up was done in the garden beside the well.)

The stone mortar will have a wooden pestle, and wood is also used for the bread-making equipment and spoons for both cooking and eating. The tripods over the hearth fire are iron, and an iron *eysiran* (spatula) is used to scrape dough from the side of the dough trough and the braziers. Trays, cups, bowls, and pans are made of enamel as are the *cezve* (Turkish coffee pots) which come in a range of sizes. Wrought or cast copper is used for pots and pans, plates and bowls, and for the round trays on which meals are served.

Meals are eaten in one of the sitting rooms rather than in the kitchen. A square linen or woven cotton tablecloth is laid on the floor and on this a trestle or round *tambour* (a circular frame) is placed. This serves as a support for the large dining tray. Wooden soup spoons are placed either around the edge of the tray or around the soup tureen in the middle of the tray. Salt and pepper dispensers are set on the tray, and a pitcher and mugs are placed nearby. Near the door, just inside the sitting room, are a basin and jug of water. The daughter of the house pours water from the jug so that guests may wash their hands before taking their place at the table.

These are the traditional utensils and customs. The old people of Sille still preserve the old ways but technological developments are beginning to infiltrate the Sille kitchen. Old utensils are being replaced by modern versions. Binnaz Saat is one of the older residents of Sille. Her house is a hundred years old and she keeps to the traditional ways, but after her death it is doubtful whether her home and kitchen will be protected as they are now.

ASIA
&
AUSTRALIA

❖

The Indian Raj   The Hindu Kitchen   Japan
Thailand   China   Sumatra and Java   Australia

THE INDIAN RAJ
A Colonial Legacy

❖

JULIE SAHNI

The influence of the Portuguese, Dutch, French, and English reshaped the traditional Indian ways of cooking and dining. The ruling powers colonized India, introduced the concept of masters and servants, and demanded a life of the utmost luxury and comfort. The native Indians provided the service required to accommodate their lifestyle.

From the sixteenth century, new buildings reflected this change in the structure of Indian life and culture. For the first time, the kitchen was designed as a separate structure, far removed from the mansion. It was strategically located close enough to ensure smooth, efficient service to those in the main house, yet far enough away to keep out what were then considered pollutants—the sounds, smells, and visible signs of servant life that would infringe upon the master's authority: this was segregation with proximity.

Each new foreign power brought changes to the kitchen. Until the coming of the Portuguese at the beginning of the sixteenth century, there was no Western-style baking done in India. The Portuguese introduced the wood-burning brick oven in which they baked bread called *pao*, which they served with sausages called *choriza*. Subsequently, the French and English brought gas and electric ovens, as well as Western ingredients, equipment, and food preparation techniques, such as roasts, grills, puddings, cakes, cookies, and tarts, all of which have since become integral elements of Indian cuisine.

The British, the last to arrive, stayed the longest—around 200 years. Their influence on Indian culture and cuisine has been the most profound. Decades after its independence from the British in 1947, India continues to cherish several Raj legacies, among them the Raj kitchen.

A traditional Raj kitchen is roomy with many built-in amenities: cooktop and oven, sink, work table, counters, and storage cabinets. Some even have an Indian clay *tandoor* for baking *naan* breads and roasting *tandoori* chicken.

The most basic of implements and equipment are used to produce one of the world's most sophisticated cuisines; the blend and balance of flavor and texture are of paramount importance. The traditional Raj kitchen (opposite) is a spacious room.

Indians have always liked to use very, very fresh ingredients when they cook. It is, therefore, not uncommon for butchering—particularly of small birds and beasts like chickens, turkeys, duck, squab, pheasant, and goats—to be carried out in the kitchen itself rather than at the market. In addition, it is traditional for the master of the house to go hunting and fishing. It is the cook's responsibility to transform the results of his expeditions into palatable delicacies. As a result, a special area close to the sink is designated for preparing meats and equipped with a butcher's table, knives, hooks, and trussing cords.

The walls of the kitchen are lined with shelves containing flavorings such as vinegars, extracts and essences, hot sauces, fragrant oils such as mustard, olive, sesame and coconut, and spices—cumin, coriander, cinnamon, clove, cardamom, and black pepper. And in one shady, cool, and airy corner of the kitchen stands a *jalidar almaira*, a screened cabinet in which perishables are stored: freshly boiled milk, fragrant clarified butter (*usli ghee*), sweet yogurt, green pickles and fresh chutney, desserts and sweetmeats, and fruits and herbs that would otherwise attract flies.

Root vegetables—onions, garlic, and potatoes—are kept in baskets hung from the ceiling, and green vegetables and herbs are purchased fresh for each meal. Preparation of the vegetables—chopping, mincing, and dicing—is now done on the counter, rather than on the floor in the traditional manner.

The Raj kitchen also contains several modern gadgets, including an egg beater, coffee grinder, cheese and vegetable grater, and an electric blender. Baking and roasting are popular cooking methods; therefore, a variety of baking pans, cookie sheets, cake tins, and mixing bowls line the kitchen cabinets or are stored on the lower shelf of the kitchen table.

The pantry, an extension of the kitchen, is an important area in the Raj household. It is as functional as the kitchen, yet as elegant as the dining room next door. It contains many locked cabinets in which the

Shelves of utensils and essential flavorings. The latter includes cooking oils such as mustard and sesame, and the vegetable-based yellow and red food colorings that give tandoori food its distinctive hue.

An array of Indian dishes. The preparation of such a feast requires careful planning and organization, and a high degree of culinary skill.

family's china, silver, linen, serving dishes, and candles are stored. On the counter tops rest small appliances, such as a bar mixer, crepe pans, toaster, waffle iron, electrical griddle, and—more recently—a microwave oven. There are hot plates to warm food brought from the kitchen.

Adjoining the pantry is a storeroom that holds supplies such as rice, flour, lentils, and sugar; liquor; dried meats, fish, fruits, nuts, and mushrooms; special spices; canned cheeses; and maraschino cherries.

The pantry is the place where the two worlds meet. Except for special occasions, the mistress of the house stays out of the kitchen and—to the cook's immense relief—out of his business. Every day, however, after the morning cup of tea, it is customary for the mistress to meet the cook in the pantry to plan and discuss the day's menu.

The mistress takes out her household accounting book and presents to the cook the menu for the day's breakfast, lunch, afternoon tea, evening cocktails, dinner, and late-night supper; they also discuss any special needs of the family. The cook quickly does calculations and specifies how much of each ingredient he requires to fulfill her menu. Accordingly the mistress measures out and gives to the cook the ingredients available in the household, and provides the money needed to buy meats, fish, and dairy products from the market. The cook then takes over and proceeds to prepare the family's food for the day.

Heavy grinding stones were vital for the preparation of sauces. Cooks developed a deftness in using them as they squatted on the ground. They have now been replaced in many households by the electric coffee grinder and blender.

The kitchen is always manned by a male cook who is of Christian or Moslem faith to allow more flexibility in the cooking. The cook, called *khansama* in India, usually has an assistant called a *masalchi*, who does all the preparational work and sometimes runs errands. Large households usually have two cooks, one to do "continental" Western-style cooking and the other to do *desi* or Indian-style cooking. Most foods are cooked in aluminum or brass pans lined with tin. An iron wok is kept for making specialties such as *kala chana*, blackened chickpeas or sour chickpeas.

All cooking tasks are performed standing up, except when the traditional grinding stones are used, when the cook will squat. Regardless of their religious faith or immersion in Western ways, all Indian cooks believe that only with these grinding stones can they achieve the proper textures for chutney and *masala*, which form the main sauces for their curries. The grinding stones are generally placed near the sink for easy cleaning and on the floor because of their enormous weight—between 20 and 100 pounds (9–45 kilograms).

As a teenager, I grew up in one such household in northern India. Once the residence of a tax collector, our house was a spacious bungalow with arched verandahs and a sprawling lawn hemmed with rose and jasmine beds at the front. In addition to several formal bedrooms, each with an enormous bathroom attached to it, we had a formal reception room, library, drawing–living room, and a dining room with an adjoining pantry and storeroom. Instead of a back porch, we had a large, fenced-in backyard dotted with mango, guava, pomegranate, and wild berry trees.

Our kitchen was located at the far side of our "compound" or courtyard, the cosiest place in the house for us to gather and relax, much like a Western family room. I remember sitting in the compound every afternoon, sipping Brook Bond Green Label Tea and munching savories: mustard green fritters, fennel-scented crepes, scrumptious kabobs with fresh mint chutney. I recall starlit evenings and moonlit buffet-style dinners of roast mutton with mint sauce; pork chops with mash; spicy cumin and cardamom-laced kabobs with earthy *roti* bread; and delicate, saffron-imbued *basmati* pilafs. Everything was fresh and piping hot because our kitchen was close by.

And it was in that Raj kitchen that I learned to prepare Western-style ice-cream; to bake plum pudding and Christmas cake; and to cook velvety, braised *korma* lamb and spicy, stewed *keema* curries in tin-lined pans. It was in a traditional Raj kitchen that I learned the secrets of blackened chickpeas, corn *roti* bread, and mutton *biryani* pilaf.

What makes a Raj kitchen so special is the fact that you will find there both grinding stones and a food processor, kept side by side. The stoic tandoor stands next to a Western stove, and silver and gold leaf *vark* are stored right next to modern tools for carving garnishes out of fruits and vegetables. The traditional Raj kitchen combines the richness of old-world cuisine and culture with the efficiency of new-world technology, giving Indian cooks the widest possible choice in the performance of their culinary art.

A spacious, well-appointed Raj kitchen (opposite top) contained a sink, work table, shelves, chopping block, grinding stones, and storage cabinets. The dining room (below) was cool and formally furnished.

THE HINDU KITCHEN
A Tribute to Indian Culture

JULIE SAHNI

Fresh green chilies, and fresh or dried red ones—all hot—are used in chutneys, seasoned oils, and spice mixtures (above). They are ground to make chili powder, often after a mild roasting which concentrates the flavor.

The tandoor oven (opposite) ranges from a pot sunk in the ground to one built into the semblance of a stove above ground. Wood or dried dung is burned to ashes in the pot, and breads are baked inside near the top, while meat is plunged into the heat on long skewers.

Food has played a significant role in Indian culture since ancient times. Sacred Vedic hymns dating back as far as 2500 B.C. describe food as a supreme god, Anna Brahma. Indeed, food was revered as the divine life-force itself. No Indian celebration, ritual, or pageant begins without first paying homage to food, and naturally all areas in which food is either prepared or consumed are considered sacred.

The traditional Hindu Brahmin kitchen has remained unchanged, despite centuries of foreign rule. Within its walls, the values and lifestyle of ancient India are strictly maintained. It is considered much like a holy temple, and the cooking is performed with loving devotion and care. It is a space in which women reign, except in large cooking establishments such as a Maharaja's palace or temple, where men—the priests—dominate.

All across India, traditional kitchens have certain common elements, as they are governed by Hindu dietary laws established by the Vedic Aryan some 4,000 years ago. The kitchen is usually a separate room, with the best natural light and ventilation in the house, though sometimes it is part of the porch along an inner courtyard or backyard. Since it will not have mechanical ventilation, it must be located where smoke will be carried away naturally on a breeze.

The Indian kitchen is starkly empty; there are no cabinets, electrical appliances or fixtures of any kind—not even a kitchen sink. The location of the well or water faucet generally governs the kitchen's location, unless water has to be brought from the center of town in jugs.

Before an Indian family moves into a new house, various rituals have to be carried out in order to bless and dedicate the kitchen. The family priest is called in to purify the space with the smoke of cinnamon and sandalwood, with sweet aromatic camphor, and with prayers. The family then builds a mud stove, called an *adupu*, out of clay, hay, and pebbles. It

Grinding spices to make the aromatic mixture known as masala, *of which there are many regional and family variations, is virtually a daily ritual.* Masala *is usually added toward the end of the cooking period, and is also used as a garnish sprinkled over the finished item. The preparation of* chapatis, parathas, *and other forms of bread is also a daily ritual.*

is customary for the family to break this stove down if it moves out of the house. Decorated with vermillion, turmeric, water, and mango leaves, the stove is then fueled with briquettes of cow dung (believed to have an antiseptic quality) and coconut husks. Next, rice is cooked in a traditional rice pot called a *vengala panai*. As the rice boils over and runs down the sides of the stove, a caste stamp is put on the entire kitchen. Once these rituals have been performed, the family will eat only food cooked on its own stove within the four walls of its own kitchen. No one outside the caste is allowed into the kitchen area or near the family's food. This rigid dietary law stems from Vedic times when the health and hygiene of the family could be secured only by excluding what were considered undesirable elements.

Each Indian family places granite grinding stones near the family well. Slightly embedded in the ground as stationary fixtures, there are two types, one called *ami* or *sil-batta*, the other *kalla oral*, both similar to the Mexican grinding stones called *metate*. An *ami* is used for pulverizing spices and herbs, while a *kalla oral* creams beans into foamy, light batters used in making feathery dumplings and lacey crepes. After each use, the grinding stones are rinsed clean and left to dry in the hot sun. In one corner of the yard, each family also keeps a *chakki*, a mill for grinding spices, legumes, grains, and other dry ingredients.

The room next to the kitchen is usually turned into the prayer room. Staples—grains, sugars, spices, clarified butter called *usli ghee*, pickles, and candies—are stored in a contained area within this prayer room.

The staples for each meal are brought into the kitchen in the platters, baskets, and bowls in which they will be mixed or chopped, since there are no kitchen counters and often the kitchen floor is finished with natural clay. As there is no refrigerator, all fresh produce and dairy products are brought to the kitchen daily, which lends dishes a sprightly, springlike flavor and also means that food must be consumed immediately.

The pots and pans, used both for storage and for cooking, are made of clay, brass, iron, blue steel, copper, and tin. In fact, some cooking utensils are expressly made out of particular materials so that when they are used they will lend a distinct flavor and character to the dish being prepared. *Kala chana*, braised black chickpeas, for example, gets its color and name from the iron pot in which it is cooked. Similarly, *appam*, a rice and coconut batter pancake, has the right texture and taste when made in the traditional earthenware pot called an *appam chetti*. And any southern Indian from Madras will tell you that to prepare an authentic *rasam*, which is a curry-laced lentil broth, it must be cooked in a zinc pot called an *eeya shomboo*.

In recent years, because of cost, convenience, and availability, stainless steel cooking utensils, metal dinner plates, drinking glasses, mechanical or electric blenders, and grinders are replacing traditional pieces in the Indian kitchen. This is an unfortunate trend as it has been well documented that traditional cooking utensils not only perform tasks brilliantly but also provide cooks with healthier, aluminum-free, cookware. Using utensils made of iron, brass, copper, and tin also ensured a regular dose of the minerals necessary for health.

The traditional cookware was beneficial to health for other reasons too. When a herb blend for a curry is ground on a grinding stone, essential minerals are released in the grinding process and worked into the final paste. Best of all, the cold stone grinding process protects volatile oils present in the herbs. For example, turmeric and salt contain essential potassium and sodium, both of which are retained when ground in this way.

Traditional Indian steaming tools, so beautifully shaped and gleaming, are possessions of which the housewife is extremely proud, and she will often treasure them to pass on as family heirlooms.

The extreme heat in India makes it imperative that food is eaten as soon as it is cooked to avoid spoilage. A typical south Indian day begins with a cup of coffee followed around 10 a.m. with lunch, the main meal of the day. The warm and humid tropical afternoons slow digestive systems and make the liver sluggish, but enticing, spicy, and pungent *tiffin*, such as banana fritters, semolina puddings, split pea griddle cakes, and wheat cakes, are all perfect as quick revitalizers. *Tiffin*, usually eaten around 2 p.m. at tea, are heavy and filling, so the evening meal is generally a light one. Steamed dumplings, delicate noodles, and airy muffins are commonly served with a bowl of soup and a salad.

I still remember visiting my grandmother's Hindu Brahmin home in Tanjore, the Holy City in south India, when I was a very small child of five. Her home was built of wood and mud plaster and was shaded by giant coconut palm, tamarind, and jackfruit trees. Jasmine, marigold, and marjoram grew in the front garden.

When we visited Grandmother, our day began long before daybreak with a ceremonial bath at the well. We used turmeric, a well-known antiseptic, as soap, and polished our teeth with charred almond shells, which were believed to remove plaque. Grandmother draped herself in a purified sari, which had been touched by no one but her. She ensured this by washing all the saris herself, spreading them out to dry on rods, and then lifting them with a makeshift pulley high up to the ceiling out of everyone's way. Grandmother kept a pot of holy basil, *tulasi*, near the well to use for our daily prayers, after which she proceeded to the kitchen.

After lighting the stove, there were other quick rituals and prayers to perform. Just about then, the milkman would bring fresh milk from his farm. Grandmother boiled the milk, so fresh that it was still warm and frothy, and combined it with freshly roasted and ground *nilgiri*, coffee beans, from the blue mountains of southern India, and palm sugar, to make the most heavenly coffee on earth.

Sitting in the corner of the kitchen, sipping saffron-flavored milk, as coffee is not offered to children until they are teenagers, I watched Grandmother attentively. She cooked lentils first, as these were the main source of protein for vegetarian Brahmins. She added a little turmeric—to "orange" the lentils—and then tamarind, chilies, and ginger.

A woman prepares a dough using ata, *a very finely ground wholewheat flour (top). Some breads are deep-fried, others are cooked in a tandoor oven, while many are baked on a tava—a heated, concave, cast-iron plate.*

Butter is churned in an earthenware pot with a whirling wooden paddle (above). Ghee, often used in Indian cooking, is a form of clarified butter made from soured buffalo or cow's milk.

As the fragrances began to fill the air, Grandmother would settle herself on the floor to work. First, she sliced vegetables—okra, eggplant (aubergine), and squash—on a vertical knife call an *aravamanai*, which she held securely with her foot. Then, with one strong whack on the grinding stone, she opened a coconut fresh from the backyard and sliced it. She scraped the sweet, fragrant coconut meat with a coconut grater called a *tenga turavi*. Next, she pounded red chili pods, tamarind, mustard, and fenugreek into a spice blend. She accomplished all of this while sitting down, but stood to execute the cooking.

We ate our meals with our fingers while we sat on the floor with our legs crossed in yoga position. It was a strict rule that we washed our hands, and sometimes even our feet, before we sat down to eat. Grandmother served our food on banana leaves, as has been done for thousands of centuries, because banana trees were so plentiful in everyone's backyard. A banana leaf was spread in front of each member of the family and rice spooned onto it. As soon as the hot rice touched the cool banana leaf, earthy scents and herbal aromas mingled with the pungent odors of tamarind and curry. Soups and brothy curries were spooned into boat-shaped cups formed out of banana leaves and secured with thin twigs. We drained water from disposable terracotta mugs, which gave the water a wonderful fragrance.

It comforts me to know that the traditional Indian kitchen still exists, even with its slight Westernization, for it is only in such an aromatic room that the spiritual power and healthy properties of the savory delicacies, whose origins date back thousands of years, can still be honored.

Women in western Bengal cook out in a courtyard using a simple tandoor oven. Zebu cattle ruminate in the background, beside a thatched wood and mud hut.

JAPAN
The Country House Kitchen

❖

RICHARD HOSKING

A *pedal-operated mortar and pestle (above) was used for husking and polishing rice, a domestic rather than agricultural operation.*

A *kettle being brought to boil over the irori (opposite), a sunken hearth usually situated in a room adjacent to the kitchen, often without any partition, but on a higher level. People sat on the floorboards around the fire to cook and eat, squatting on thin mats. With luck, the smoke drifted up into the roof and out through the eaves.*

Imagine a valley running between mountains covered with cedar or pine, ricefields reaching to the foothills from either side of a stream, and not an animal in sight. Of course there are wild boar among those trees and monkeys in their branches, but no sheep or cattle graze, nor is there any sign of a horse.

Toward the foothills you see some thatched roofs gathered together inside a walled earthen platform. This is a house, though it appears to be several, for rather than enlarging an existing dwelling as the family grows, the Japanese usually build another one and link them together, always within the same walled area. The house appears charming from a distance, but at closer range its rather dark, enclosed appearance becomes evident. Once inside the house, the Japanese are not interested in looking out and, indeed, in a traditional house you cannot, unless for the sake of trying to catch a summer breeze you remove the sliding walls, covered with opaque white paper.

If you enter at the front, you will remove your shoes and go up inside, where the floor of the various rooms consists of *tatami*, wooden frames of a standard size covered with woven grass matting and fitted together. If, however, you go to the family entrance at the side or back, you will go into an area, *doma*, which, although sometimes paved with flagstones, is usually just compacted earth. Here you will find great stone mortars with their huge wooden pestles operated by a treadle mechanism. These are for husking and polishing rice, not for pounding pastes or grinding powders. Peer deeper into the gloom and you will see among the jumble of baskets, wooden buckets, and huge pottery water jars, the kitchen range, *kamado*, the heart of the Japanese kitchen, and in times past, the heart of the home itself.

Move further in and you will come to the floor of the house, about 2 feet (60 centimeters) above the ground. Here you must take off your shoes and enter the house proper barefooted, for outdoor footwear is not allowed in the raised part of the house.

In the traditional home, most cooking was done in the family room at the irori *(sunken hearth).*

The kamado *(opposite) was the focal point of the traditional Japanese kitchen. Now almost completely superseded by the electric automatic rice-cooker, it is still sometimes used in country areas when large quantities of rice need to be steamed or soup made. Here on the right ordinary rice is being cooked in a traditional* kama *and on the left is a two-tiered bamboo steamer for steaming glutinous rice. Firewood and kindling are stored in readiness for use in an* irori *(above) ·*

Having removed your shoes and gone from the *doma* up onto the wooden floor, you find yourself in the family living–dining area. There is no wall between this and the kitchen area, the only difference being one of level: the ground level is the earth floor of the kitchen, and the raised boarded level is that of the living–dining area. Cooking is done in both areas, for in the middle of the floor of the living–dining area is a square opening filled with ash. This is the *irori*. Immediately above it is a device for suspending a large iron cooking pot. Once the fire is built in this space, food will be cooked in the pot, and other ingredients, especially fish, will be skewered and staked in the fireplace sufficiently near the embers to cook through.

So within one space we have the family's living–dining area centered on the *irori*, around which the family will squat without any table for their meals; and the lower, compacted earth area, the true kitchen, centering on the *kamado*.

Traditionally the *kamado* was seen as the center of family life, and setting up a new branch of the family was called "dividing the *kamado*." Nowadays the *kamado*'s work has almost completely been taken over by the electric rice-cooker, for cooking rice was the main function of the *kamado*. It was a very efficient structure usually built of clay and lime, sometimes of brick or stone, to house the fire for cooking rice and other

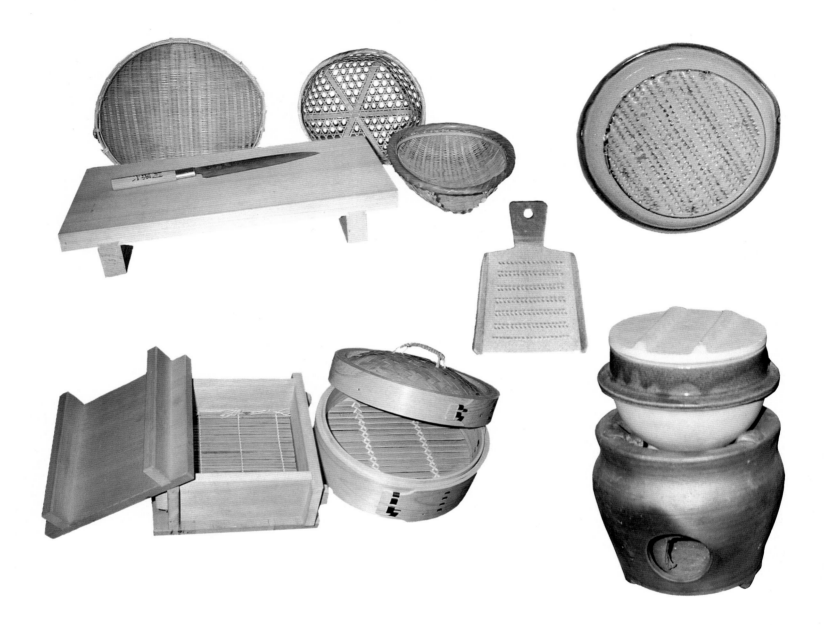

A *selection of kitchen utensils. A good chopping board, preferably on struts, is the first essential of Japanese cooking (top left). Next is a good sharp knife. Baskets used as colanders are also needed in various shapes and sizes. The grater (top right) is made of pottery, the square steamer of wood and the round steamer of bamboo. The* shichirin *(charcoal burner) on the right is supporting an individual rice-cooker for making* kamameshi *(pot rice), a dish of rice cooked with other ingredients such as seafood, mushrooms, or chestnuts. Old Japanese houses are so drafty there is never any danger from the fumes.*

foods that might be cooked in the big pots that fitted snugly into the top of the *kamado*. The pots had heavy wooden lids, since it is important not to let steam escape while rice is cooking. The fire was fueled by wood and there was usually provision for two or three pots. Large families needed more, and then the *kamado* would be curved so that one person could watch all the fires at the same time. Usually separate from the main *kamado* there was another very large one, used only a few times a year to make *miso* (fermented bean paste) and *mochi* (glutinous rice cakes) for festivals. The outside of the *kamado* became shiny from being constantly wiped with a cloth.

Grilling was usually done on a portable clay brazier—the *shichirin*—using charcoal. In the living area, another kind of brazier, the *hibachi*, was used for warming hands in winter, for Japanese houses are perishingly cold.

All the peeling, slicing, and chopping that goes into the preparation of a Japanese meal was normally done standing at a wooden bench, working on a sturdy chopping board possibly raised on struts of wood and using a variety of knives sharper than swords. The knives, of course, were sharpened on whetstones of varying degrees of fineness. There was no other way, especially as the knives were only sharpened on one face. Sometimes, instead of using a workbench, part of the *doma* was covered with floorboards and the housewife would kneel on that in order to prepare the food.

As well as fire, a kitchen needs water, not only for cooking but also for washing vegetables and cleaning cooking and eating utensils. In the traditional Japanese kitchen stood a huge pottery jar filled with water from the well. Vegetables and utensils were washed in a shallow wooden trough against the outer wall. An outlet through to the outside of the

Dumplings are most often steamed or poached, but these oyaki *dumplings are being baked in the hot ashes of a spent fire.*

This pickling room contains all the equipment necessary for making miso *and pickles, an important part of any Japanese meal. They are vegetable pickles and not intended for long storage. Steamers for preparing the grain and soya beans for* miso *fermentation, baskets for washing vegetables, and tubs and crocks for making and storing pickles are all stored here.*

A wooden washing-up trough (opposite) is carved from a large log. Cold water comes in through a pipe, and utensils are stored on shelves in the window.

house drained the dirty water away. To this day, most Japanese do their washing-up in cold water, so there was no need for any means of making water hot.

Apart from the big mortar and knives already mentioned, there were a stone hand-mill mostly used for making soya bean flour, and a finer one for making green tea powder; and, of course, a *kama*, the heavy-duty pot for cooking rice. This had a flange around the middle, so that when it was placed on the *kamado* it fitted snugly and no heat escaped. There were other pots, also for use on the *kamado* and for hanging over the *irori*, as well as some square wooden and round bamboo steaming baskets. Other kitchen utensils included large cooking chopsticks, soup ladles, wooden spoons, including special ones for serving rice, *suribachi* (a pottery mortar, ridged inside, used especially for grinding sesame seeds), *tawashi* (stiff fiber brushes used for cleaning pans and scrubbing vegetables), graters of various shapes and sizes—a very fine one for *wasabi* (Japanese horseradish) and ginger, and a coarser one for grating *daikon* (white radish). These graters were usually made of pottery or bamboo. Mention must also be made of an intriguing device called a *katsuobushibako*—a tool for shaving *katsuobushi*, the fillet of the bonito fish dried until it was as hard as wood. A plane was fitted upside-down into the top of a box, and when the *katsuobushi* was pulled over it, the shavings fell into a drawer in the bottom of the box. These shavings were boiled in water, usually with dried seaweed, to make a very delicate soup stock. The family cat also enjoyed its share of bonito shavings.

The traditional kitchen was not a tidy place, especially in the country, where the farmer's wife was too busy working in the fields to be tidying up the kitchen all the time. In *The Essential Japanese House* Teiji Itoh observes that

> *The disorderly assemblage of household utensils and farming tools is hardly in keeping with the fabled neatness of Japanese interiors so often praised in the West, but the average Japanese farmer and his family are too preoccupied with making a living to trouble themselves about superficialities. Besides, as the visitor to Japan quickly discovers, the Japanese passion for neatness has been considerably exaggerated by over-enthusiastic foreign observers.*

Only the rich can afford the luxury of beautiful, understated, furnitureless rooms. Most Japanese live in houses where there is nowhere to put anything and the kitchen is no exception. In the traditional house the kitchen windows, if not simply of open wooden slats, were glazed with frosted glass or fitted with sliding paper panels. Across the windows, shelves were fitted for storage of pots and pans.

As for the smoke from the various fires, it simply found its way up to the sooty rafters and out through spaces under the roof. It was not surprising, then, that offerings were usually left near the *kamado* to *Kojin*, the god of fire, for if he were not properly respected he might get angry and burn the house down. From the facts of daily life in Japan, it seems that he was often angry!

THAILAND
Traditional Rural Kitchens

❖

PHILIP IDDISON

Over many centuries Thai homes have been built of wood, more permanent materials being reserved for temples. In the tropical climate very few of these old homes have survived, even in fragmentary form. One cannot find and inspect a typical kitchen built say two centuries ago, as one might be able to do in another country. However, Thai culture has been very stable since it developed from its various ethnic roots in about the thirteenth century. Temple murals often depict domestic scenes among the epic stories and from this evidence it would appear that culinary practice has changed little over the last few centuries.

The simple kitchens still seen in the countryside therefore give a good impression of the form of kitchens in the past. Until quite recently, in fact, even luxury villas in Bangkok suburbs were often fitted out with a large but basic maid's kitchen, complete with concrete slabs for charcoal braziers. The current vogue for condominiums will inevitably bring rapid change and encourage the adoption of the Western-style kitchen in the cities of Thailand.

In the traditional house compound, the kitchen (*kroew fai*) is a small separate building: a sensible precaution when most construction is still of wood. It is often on the edge of the raised platform occupied by the several units that make up the family home. In the simplest village home, built entirely of bamboo, the verandah is both the kitchen and the eating area. Such a small home belonging to a rice farmer also has a granary next to the kitchen as only the rice harvest in excess of the family's needs for food and seed is ever sold.

A typical rural kitchen in a medium-sized house is well ventilated to disperse smoke and help preserve dried goods. The hearth is a wooden box (*tao fai*) filled with earth on which a cooking tripod supports the pots. Wood or charcoal is used as fuel, and above the hearth a storage rack (*hing*) holds baskets in the smoke to discourage insect attack.

A cook at work in a traditional wooden Thai house (above). Steaming and stir-frying are the main cooking methods employed in Thailand.

A stone pestle and mortar (opposite) are essential for making curry pastes, ingredients for which frequently include chilies, lemon grass, kaffir limes and their leaves, galangal, and coriander (cilantro) leaves and roots.

Fresh ingredients and careful preparation are the keys to success in Thai cooking.

The rural floating markets of Damnoensaduak, a half-day excursion from Bangkok, have an abundance of snacks and staple ingredients on offer (opposite).

The daily rice is pounded to remove the husk in a large wooden mortar half-buried in the ground adjacent to the house, and steamed in a conical basket or wooden vessel with a bottom vent and stopper.

Fresh food is collected daily from field and forest, or purchased in the market, to supplement basic stocks of dried and preserved goods, such as rice or fish sauce. Water is kept in large earthenware jars; heat is provided by a charcoal brazier; a thick block of tamarind wood serves as a preparation surface; and a small selection of cleavers takes care of the cutting. A substantial pestle and an earthenware, wooden, or stone mortar are essential, together with a selection of basketry, metal, and pottery cooking and serving vessels. Chopping, shredding, pounding, and mixing are done on the floor, with the cook kneeling or sitting cross-legged to the task. A box of crushed ice might be on hand to keep fish and meat fresh and drinks cool. There is no call for refrigerator, food processor, oven, sink, or table!

The kitchen is also used for preparing preserved food, an important aspect of rural Thai cuisine where any seasonal excess must be stored as part of the frugal home economy. Thus small fish are salted in earthenware jars (*pla raa*) as a condiment and their larger brethren are sun-dried (*pla haeng*) for later consumption.

A curious example of the art of carving from Chiang Mai in the north of Thailand. The bowl of the spoon is fashioned from coconut.

Cooking in the home is still the work of female servants or the women of a family. Food preparation involves much intricate effort on a great variety of ingredients. For the more complex dishes a curry paste will be ground freshly and individually for each dish, and vegetables intricately carved either as ingredients or for garnish. Dishes are typically assembled just before serving and often require only the briefest cooking. A special meal may involve many dishes. Most of the food will be served practically cold, a practice that suits a cuisine where the fire is often provided by the liberal use of chilies or fresh root ginger.

The first meal of the day is usually a rice gruel soup (*jok*) enlivened with a little chicken, squid, or dried fish. In rural communities a large portion of rice (*khao*) will be steamed for the day, eaten hot for breakfast, and taken to the fields in a basket for a cold lunch. Townsfolk will often lunch at a street or market foodstall. With sundown the family reassembles for a more complex meal, perhaps a soup (*gaeng chud*), a salad (*yam*), a curry (*gaeng*), and more rice. For men, the evening may devolve into a session of drinks and snacks (*kab klaem*) with acquaintances at a favorite restaurant.

Many of the utensils in the cook's room are still craft items, whether made in the home in which they are used, or taken to market for sale. There is an astonishing range of basketwork: trays are used for drying food or winnowing grain; strainers are woven to prepare coconut milk; cooked rice containers have lids and carrying straps; small split-bamboo tables are used for serving food; and the plates themselves might be closely woven baskets. Basketry also forms the basis for the lacquerware that was very popular before modern materials became available.

Coconut shell provides a ready-made curvature for spoons, ladles, and dippers. Bamboo branches and cane are also ingeniously crafted into spoons. Wood has a multitude of uses: carved in animal form and furnished with a sharp metal tongue it becomes a coconut scraper; it is fashioned into low tables, stools, plates, and bowls; and a wooden storage cabinet may be the only substantial piece of furniture in the otherwise sparsely furnished kitchen.

Firebricks are cemented into metal buckets to make braziers; unglazed clay pots keep water cool; and glazed pottery is a long-established Thai industry. Metalwork ranges from plain steel for frying pans (*kata*), through enamelware to finely wrought and polished bronzeware for ladles and cutlery. The Thais traditionally eat with fork and spoon, and managed to survive a period of using aluminum spoons and forks, the latter ending up like metal spaghetti after every meal! Happily stainless steel is now in vogue, though in the north, where glutinous rice is the popular staple cereal, eating directly with the hand, dipping a ball of rice into a communal dish, is still the norm.

Today, as always, the cook's domain in Thailand, is still a simple space wherein great skill, basic equipment, and an abundance of time make Thai cookery appear a leisurely activity.

A cook (previous pages) sits cross-legged at her task of chopping and pounding, surrounded by a profusion of eggplant, long beans, and varieties of squash.

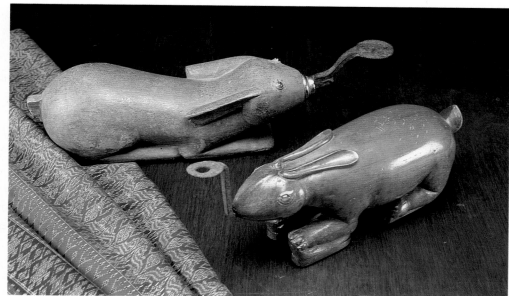

It would be understandable if one were simply to enjoy looking at these wares rather than use them. The platter and jar are from the Sukhothai period. In the thirteenth century, the Thais rebelled against their distant Khmer rulers and set up an independent kingdom, with the city of Sukhothai (meaning the Dawn of Happiness) as its capital. The teapot and bowl are examples of old Bencharong wares. The basket and coconut graters carved in the form of rabbits are further examples of traditional Thai craftsmanship.

CHINA
Kitchens of Economy

C LIO W HITTAKER

Perhaps because hunger has all too frequently been a way of life throughout China's history, food is a subject of great interest to the Chinese. The mouth-watering relish with which details of banquets are recounted in early literature is evidence that eating has long been a refined art. And yet, despite the importance attached to food and eating, the kitchen is usually to be found in one of the least significant corners of the house.

All Chinese buildings—whether temples or houses—are made up of rectangular-shaped buildings. A simple house, typical of north China, is a single-storey building with windows on the south-facing side only, giving onto a square walled courtyard. The central entrance door leads into a space that functions as corridor, utility area, and kitchen. The side rooms are usually allocated according to seniority in the family, with the eastern bedroom generally reserved for the older generation. This room is the center of family life, serving as reception and dining area, as well as a place for sleeping. A dwelling for a richer or larger family follows the same basic layout, but with additional structures along the sides of the courtyard. These rooms receive less direct sunlight, so the most important rooms—the ancestral hall in a large compound, or the main living area in a modest home—are those that face due south. The projecting eaves that are so characteristic of Chinese buildings provide shelter from the sun around the edges of the courtyard and create a dry passage between the separate areas in rainy weather.

Affluent family living in a compound with several structures built around courtyards arranged one behind the other, will observe the principle of *qiantang houshi* (main rooms at the front, private rooms behind). The cooking area is relegated to a peripheral zone of the house, to the rear or in the side wings.

Chinese houses are usually simply decorated and furnished, and the kitchen, *chufang*, is no exception. This small and poorly lit space will probably have bare walls and a floor of tamped earth. The only

Fodder is left to dry around a simple, brightly colored building in north China (above).

Because of its cold climate, north China produces and consumes little rice. Wheat, millet, barley, and sorghum are grown on the alluvial plains, and steam-cooked bread rolls and flat bread are eaten as an accompaniment in place of rice (opposite).

A large, solid zao *(top). Eighty percent of the cook's preparation time is likely to be taken up with tasks such as trimming off fat, soaking dried and salted foodstuffs, and cutting all the ingredients into pieces of the same size, both to ensure even cooking and to give the finished dish an attractive appearance. A* wok *(above) enables small pieces of food to be cooked rapidly without absorbing too much fat; hence the popularity of stir-frying among health-conscious Westerners. A single Chinese dish may require two or more cooking processes to achieve the desired result. For example, food may be fried raw and then refried with a coating applied; or it may be boiled before it is stir-fried or deep-fried.*

furnishings are a simple wooden cupboard and a few shelves for storing crockery, condiments, and utensils. Meals are rarely consumed in the kitchen, so not even table and chairs are necessary.

The largest and most important feature in a traditional Chinese kitchen is undoubtedly the stove. A typical stove, *zao*, consists of a brick box 2 or 3 feet (60–90 centimeters) high, and up to 6 feet (1.8 meters) square, with a small opening at ground level into the cavity in which fuel is burned. Pots fit snugly into holes cut in the top of the stove, ensuring that heat loss from the surface is minimized.

In north China fuel is scarce, so what fuel there is, often just twigs and straw, is used as efficiently as possible. The flue from the stove is led under the *kang*, the raised brick platform bed that can take up as much as half the room space of north China dwellings. The *kang* is not used only for sleeping. During the day the padded bed quilts are neatly folded and it becomes a warm and congenial gathering place for the family, the center of all activity and even used for food preparation. During the summer months and in the warmer climate of southern China, stoves are not needed for heating, so they can be located outside either in the open or under a simple shelter. Smaller portable pottery or metal stoves that burn briquettes made of coal dust are common in the south and in cities, although newly built dwellings have gas burners.

Of the various gods that traditionally were believed to protect the home from evil and misfortune, *Zaojun*, the kitchen or stove god, was probably the most intimately involved with the household's affairs. A paper image or small statue of this most approachable deity was pasted on the wall of the cooking area or placed in a niche behind the stove. The women, particularly the daughters-in-law and unmarried daughters of the house, who bore the responsibility for most of the cooking and other domestic chores, brought him news of all the important events in the family. At New Year his lips were smeared with honey to ensure that he uttered only sweet words when he made his annual report to heaven on the family's conduct. Then the soot-blackened image was burnt to give *Zaojun* a good send-off. Although such superstitious practices are now frowned upon, many rural homes still give house room to this deity.

In the traditional kitchen there are few cooking utensils, and these are mostly handmade. The round-bottomed frying pan widely known by its Cantonese name, *wok*, is the most familiar of these. Although early woks were probably made of pottery, they are now made of cast iron or aluminum. Their curved sides distribute heat evenly through the vessel and ensure that the liquid evaporates quickly. A wok is essential to the technique of stir-frying, in which food is cooked for a few minutes only at a very high temperature—a method developed from the need to use as little fuel as possible.

A deeper pot with a cover is used for boiling and steaming. It is usually made of metal nowadays, but it, too, was originally made of earthenware. Bamboo baskets with slatted bottoms fit over this pot, so that rice can be cooked in the bottom while a variety of other foods are

steamed in the bamboo baskets stacked on top. Basketware and brooms were once fashioned during periods of slack agricultural activity and in many rural areas their sale provided a significant proportion of the family income. Today, in the cities and increasingly in the countryside, traditional handcrafted utensils are being superseded by implements mass-produced in urban factories.

Stir-frying, boiling, and steaming are the most common methods of cooking in China, but by no means the only ones at the disposal of the Chinese cook. As many as forty different techniques have been identified, and for some of these special pots are needed. The Mongolian hotpot, for example, consists of a U-shaped ring that fits around a tall chimney in which charcoal is burned. Wafer-thin slices of meat and vegetables are dipped into water boiling in the ring, allowed to cook briefly, then eaten. The water gradually takes on the flavors of the ingredients to become a delicious soup which is then consumed at the end of the meal.

Cooking may be done over a portable metal stove with woks and cooking pots balanced in the center. The metal ladles used to turn the food while it cooks are often shallower than their European versions, corresponding to the curve of the wok.

Since the equipment needed to prepare a meal is simple and portable, in summer much of the food preparation takes place outside in the courtyard; and in winter the warm *kang* becomes more congenial than the kitchen area. For some dishes, such as dumplings, the whole family might join in the work. In almost all cases, it takes longer to prepare the ingredients than it does to cook the dish. A cleaver is used with great dexterity to perform all tasks that require a knife: a section of tree trunk, which can easily be moved around depending on where the food is being prepared, acts as work surface and chopping board. Meat and vegetables are cut into small pieces of uniform size—cubes, slices, shreds—so that the ingredients will cook quickly and evenly.

With the exception of fruit, food is never eaten raw in China—a wise precaution since human nightsoil is widely used as a fertilizer. Likewise, water is always boiled and either drunk hot or made into tea. The vacuum flask for hot water is a universal piece of equipment in Chinese homes. In the past, water would be drawn at a village or communal well, and carried back to the house to be stored in a large covered earthenware jar. In the cities, water could be bought from the water-seller as he pushed his wheelbarrow through the streets.

Preparing and cooking food outdoors is preferable during the summer months, or if one's job is too far from home to warrant returning for lunch or a quick meal. A small portable stove is easily conveyed to the work place.

The process of steaming is used to cook some breads and dumplings (above). The latter are often stuffed with finely chopped meat and are but one of the many morsels that comprise the famous Cantonese dim sum, *which means "to dot the heart." The Mandarin term,* tien hsin, *translates as "the heart touchers." Because bamboo steamers are porous, excess moisture is prevented from condensing inside the lid and dripping onto the food being cooked.*

Noodle makers (opposite top) like to make great show of their dexterity in wielding the long lengths of dough. Egg noodles, mung bean flour noodles (cellophane noodles), and rice noodles come in many sizes. A cook copes cheerfully with a swirling mass of steam (opposite below).

A rural community might have had a mill for husking rice or grinding grain in bulk but for those without access to draft animals the task had to be done by hand. Preserved foods were, and still are, stored in barrel-shaped earthenware jars of all sizes, glazed in shades of brown and green. Most are sealed with a simple earthenware lid, but an ingenious and early way of achieving an airtight seal was to have a water-filled trough inside the rim of the jar with a lid fitting over the top.

The regional variations in Chinese cuisine are a close reflection of the geography and climate of the different areas. Thus, south of the Yangzi River, where rainfall is high and summers hot and long, the growing season can last nine or ten months. Fast-maturing strains of rice enable two or three crops a year to be grown, and a wide variety of fruit and vegetables. Since very little land is available for grazing in inner China, animals raised for meat are those that can be fed from household scraps, such as pigs, or scavengers, such as poultry. North of the Yangzi rainfall is less predictable and winters bitterly cold, so maize and wheat are the staple crops. The grasslands that border on Mongolia provide pasture for sheep and cattle. Here mutton and beef are prominent in the diet and dairy produce is popular. Elsewhere in China milk is generally considered repulsive and consumed by babies and old people only. Since neither refrigeration nor transport is common or advanced in China, food is bought or gathered daily and what is eaten is governed by what is seasonally available.

Food is served as soon as it comes off the heat, with dish after dish filling up the table; thus the person cooking is generally unable to take part in the meal he or she has prepared. An everyday meal for most Chinese will consist of a large quantity of a staple—rice, noodles, or steamed bread depending on the region—enlivened by a dish or two based on vegetables with a small amount of meat, fish or eggs, and followed by a soup. A well-planned Chinese meal is designed to present a harmonious balance of contrasts—of tastes, colors, textures, and ingredients. The medicinal qualities of foods will also be taken into account, and whether the constituents are *yin* or *yang*, the ancient Chinese dualistic concepts of light and dark, male and female, hot and cold.

The table is as simply furnished as the kitchen. The minimum equipment for each member of the family is a small bowl, a spoon, and a pair of chopsticks. Since all the ingredients have already been cut into pieces of easily manageable size, there has never been a need for a knife. Food is often served straight from the pot or the basket in which it has been steamed, although larger serving plates or bowls are kept to offer hospitality to guests.

Like the land itself, Chinese cuisine encompasses a great range of contrasts. It shares some of the characteristics of the Chinese method of agriculture in that natural resources are used sparingly and a great deal of time and energy is spent in the preparation. These distinctive features and attitudes can also be seen in the simple and economical appearance of the Chinese kitchen.

SUMATRA AND JAVA
The Kitchens of Indonesia

SRI OWEN

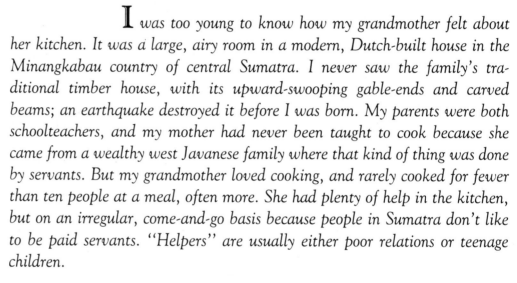

I *was too young to know how my grandmother felt about her kitchen. It was a large, airy room in a modern, Dutch-built house in the Minangkabau country of central Sumatra. I never saw the family's traditional timber house, with its upward-swooping gable-ends and carved beams; an earthquake destroyed it before I was born. My parents were both schoolteachers, and my mother had never been taught to cook because she came from a wealthy west Javanese family where that kind of thing was done by servants. But my grandmother loved cooking, and rarely cooked for fewer than ten people at a meal, often more. She had plenty of help in the kitchen, but on an irregular, come-and-go basis because people in Sumatra don't like to be paid servants. "Helpers" are usually either poor relations or teenage children.*

My grandmother was a rich woman, farming her portion of the family's lands, growing most of our food within a few minutes' walk of the house. What she didn't grow she bought every morning in the market, so storage was no problem unless one of her own animals had been slaughtered for a feast. It was spitted and roasted whole, out in the yard beyond the kitchen door where, in fine weather, most of the cooking was done anyway. A goat would be eaten at a sitting, with perhaps a few leftovers for next day, but an ox or a buffalo would produce a surplus that had to be preserved, either by making it into *rendang* or by slicing it thinly, marinating the slices and drying them in the sun to make *dendeng*.

Making *rendang* takes a bit of time and trouble even in a modern kitchen, and my grandmother worked hard on it. Her kitchen, indoors, was not unlike a prosperous English farmhouse kitchen of the seventeenth century, except that it was not a center for family life; people didn't gather there to eat or gossip. It had a floor of beaten earth (though most of the other rooms were tiled; in a Dutch colonial family, I suppose *mevrouw*—the wife—wouldn't have gone in there unless to give orders). There was a brick and stone worktop around three sides, with a cavity

Buyers of the spices and seasonings essential to Indonesian cooking have a vast range from which to choose, among them saffron, cloves, tamarind, chilies, and garlic (above). A kitchen in Sendang, Semanggi village, Bantul, Yogyakarta, Central Java (opposite).

220

Rice, the staple in Indonesia, is often accompanied by richly aromatic chicken, pork, and seafood dishes. Cooking is done in the ubiquitous wok, and frequently fueled by wood fires (top). Wok balanced over a simple transportable brazier (above).

under it for a wood fire and round holes above the fire where pans could heat. Fires could be built under all three worktops but in practice only one was used. The area beneath the other two was used for storing woks and other large pans. Small cooking fires could also be improvised on top of the work surface, or better still out in the yard, by stacking up bricks to make little barbecue-like enclosures called *tungku*. Wood, which was plentiful on her own land, was the only fuel my grandmother ever used.

I visited Clarke Hall in Wakefield, England, a few years ago and felt immediately at home in the kitchen there, surrounded by the same kind of work surfaces, although of course our kitchen did not have a big fireplace, with a cavernous chimney and its apparatus of spitjacks and trivets. People in most parts of Indonesia don't cook joints of meat or roast poultry whole, so they don't need such things. Or to put it the other way round, they don't build kitchen ranges with big chimneys, which aren't needed in the tropics and would use far too much fuel, and therefore they don't cook that way. Meat and vegetables are usually cut up before they are cooked, and *rendang* is no exception.

So my grandmother had a hefty chopping board on her worktop, and some large iron knives which were kept exceedingly clean and sharp, usually by a male member of the household since she believed, and persuaded me, that it is unlucky for a woman to sharpen a knife. When the meat was cut up, it went into a heavy iron pan where it disappeared beneath white coconut milk into which she dropped crushed chilies and turmeric. The *rendang* heaved and bubbled on the fire for an hour or two, until the sauce was a rich brown and the smell very inviting. Then everything was transferred to a massive iron wok, and the boiling and bubbling continued for a further hour, or two, or even three, while the water in the coconut milk evaporated or was absorbed into the meat, and eventually the meat was no longer boiling but frying in the sauce, which had become a spice-rich oil. My grandmother stirred and turned it

Woman pounding grain in a rough form of mortar and pestle. The implements and the technique have remained unchanged for centuries.

Eels must be kept alive until just before cooking. If not, their flesh will soften and taste unappetizing. An Indonesian specialty comprises eels fried in butter and served with vegetables and peanut sauce.

vigorously, until at last all the liquid was absorbed; the rather tough buffalo meat was by then tender and succulent, and its color almost black. Meat cooked like this not only tastes delicious, but will keep, even in the tropics, for at least a week, provided it is reheated every couple of days or so. Needless to say, my grandmother had no fridge.

Those days are half a century in the past. In spite of her prosperous life in the traditional matrilineal society of central Sumatra, my grandmother was a subject of the Queen of the Netherlands; my parents spoke Dutch together (since they came from different islands) and ate with Dutch knives and forks off Dutch porcelain. (The other members of the household, including myself, preferred to eat with our fingers as we squatted on the mat-covered bamboo platform in the room adjoining the kitchen.) It seems, and indeed is, a vanished world. The pace of change accelerates, and foodways are affected as much as any other aspect of life.

Kitchen implements and cooking pots show this perhaps better than anything else. My grandmother's were massive and very heavy. She had a big iron saucepan for cooking rice—the rice was always what we call *nasi tanak* in Sumatra, or in Java *nasi liwet*: boiled, not steamed, with a thick crust of half-burnt rice sticking to the thick bottom of the pan. This crust, the *kerak* or *intip*, was carefully prised out, dried in the sun and fried to make delicious snacks. For stews and *gulai* she had a round-bottomed earthenware pot called *belanga*, whose inside surface soon became glazed and sealed by the juices of all that she cooked in it. For deep-frying she had a huge iron wok, and for boiling water a majestically massive kettle—I think, a Dutch-style copper kettle, though probably all these items were locally made. The house had a piped water supply, though I am sure *her* mother had fetched water from the well; there was also a regular garbage collection, although most of the kitchen rubbish was organic and was therefore buried in a large pit some distance from the house. A weekly bonfire consumed any rubbish that would burn; its ashes were used for scouring greasy pans. In short, it was taken for granted that a well-to-do household on good farming land would be more or less self-supporting.

However, remembering other kitchens in houses that I lived in later, with my parents and sisters after we moved to Java, and looking now at the kitchens my sisters have in the cities where they live and work as members of the new Indonesian middle class, I wonder whether so much has changed. In a small, newish government-issue house in Jakarta, the kitchen still has the brick-and-stone workbench, though it no longer has a space under it for a wood fire; cooking is still done on the *anglo*, the Javanese charcoal stove, but also on portable electric rings or hotplates, for this house has enough watts to run a hotplate or two as well as a fridge. And the family's rice, the basis of every meal, is cooked in a Japanese electric rice-steamer, surely one of the most beneficent inventions ever to come off a drawing-board.

In Jakarta, too, I meet old school friends who have become wealthy; their kitchens are all-electric, even with electric ovens. I don't recall my

Cooking sugar to a toffee-like consistency. The cultivation of sugar cane gradually spread to Indonesia following the discovery of the New World. Sugar has come to be associated with confectionery and cake-making, but is also used for seasoning meats and savory items.

grandmother having an oven, though ladies of my mother's generation, who enjoyed Dutch-style sweet cakes, frequently did. My mother's was typical: it was a metal box with a door into which you slid two trays of glowing charcoal, top and bottom; it was always used out of doors, and with careful management it was very effective. I dare say there are still some of these devices around today. There are certainly many people who still cook on kerosene stoves, as I did at the start of my married life: a three-burner which I recall with loathing. Charcoal is safe, a clean, agreeable substance to touch, and burns without smell. Kerosene fails on all these counts, but it is easy to light and it's cheap.

If you go outside the cities, of course, you will find village houses still very much as they were fifty or a hundred years ago, except that there are now plastic utensils and aluminum or enamel pans. Kitchens in village houses still have floors of beaten earth, and people still go outside to cook and wash dishes when it's not raining. In Pontianak, in west Kalimantan, one of my sisters has a stainless steel double-drainer sink unit with running hot water, but I noticed the young helper, who washes up for her, taking a basin of water onto the back porch and doing the dishes there.

It's easy to assume that change can only go one way, and that as time passes Indonesian kitchens will simply become more like kitchens everywhere else. Presumably servants will vanish, as they have vanished from Europe within living memory. The kitchen will no longer be the link between servants and "the family." But it will still need to be as large and airy as space allows—particularly as the housewife, and often her husband as well, will be spending time in there, cooking. And in the tropics there will always be a need for the wide back porch with its lean-to roof and the yard beyond, where the charcoal stove can be carried and the cook take advantage of any breeze that blows.

AUSTRALIA
A Pioneer Settler's Kitchen

JUDY WHITE

The original kitchen on the Belltrees estate, in the Hunter Valley, New South Wales, was built in 1836, forty-eight years after the First Fleet landed in Sydney Cove and brought the first white settlers to the shores of the Australian continent. It was not until 1822 that the Colonial Secretary in London permitted settlers to take up grants of land in the Hunter Valley, some 200 miles (320 kilometers) due north of Sydney. In 1831 James White, a pioneer settler from Somerset, England, acquired a block of 1,280 acres (518 hectares) in the region; he also had unrestricted use of the unfenced land that stretched for hundreds of miles along the Hunter River.

Belltrees became an outstation, an independent settlement in which James White was responsible for the employment and care of his convict and ex-convict workforce. The site of the settlement was determined by the availability of water. For seventy years, from 1836 to 1906, the White family lived in a colonial Georgian house near the Hunter River. The convicts who built the house from sandstock bricks, baked from the clay soil on the estate, followed their employer's descriptions of similar houses in England. The design was a simple one in which windows, containing small rectangular panes of glass, were symmetrically spaced on either side of a central door.

The cook's room, which evolved from the basic needs of the pioneering family, was actually a kitchen block, built of the same material as the rest of the house, but separated from the main building because, in this hot climate, it was not uncommon for kitchens with open fireplaces to catch fire. The block consisted of the kitchen, which contained two fireplaces, and an annex, which was joined to the kitchen by a small corridor. The cook needed the annex to escape from the heat generated by the open-cooking methods. Heavy iron pots, brought from England by sailing ships, hung by chains over one large log fire. Here the meat—and, in winter, the soups and stews—were cooked. Over the other fireplace a heavy black urn of water, filled from the water butt outside the kitchen door, was kept boiling to satisfy the constant demands for tea. The temperature was regulated by the size of the fire.

For the inveterate tea drinker, the large black urn above the open fire (above) ensured a steady supply of boiling water. The battered billy can above the fireplace was also used for boiling up water, usually by the campfire. The view across the kitchen (opposite) affords a glimpse of part of the original homestead.

Fresh damper stands beside the butter churn and butter ballers (overleaf). The meat safe on the right-hand side of the room helped keep food cool and free from flies.

Wood-fired oven with cast-iron cooking pots. The large pot on the floor was used for stewing meat. Heavy-duty kitchen equipment was imported to Australia from Europe throughout the nineteenth century; the first open-hearth steel was not poured in New South Wales until 1901.

In the center of the kitchen was a large scrubbed wooden table where the cook prepared the food and rolled the dough. Food was simple. Bags of flour and sugar, and chests of tea, had to be brought hundreds of miles from the seaports by bullock waggons. The roads were rough, unmade tracks and the rivers flooded frequently, so the journey could take several weeks. Because Belltrees was so far from markets, the staple diet was bread, or damper, and meat. Damper—a scone mixture of flour and water, or flour and milk—was baked in the oven in the outside wall; the bread, which required a steady, even heat, was baked only once a week.

When the master and men rode off for their day's work in the bush they took with them sandwiches of damper and meat. These were packed into the saddlebags that hung on the near side of the saddle; quart-pots for tea were hung on the off-side. As they boiled their quart-pots on a small fire, the men would carefully unwrap the tea and sugar that had been packed in calico bags. Over the years the lunch pack of the boundary rider has altered little; he still takes his corned beef sandwiches in his saddlebag that hangs, along with his quart-pot, on the saddle. In the convict days quart-pots were often made by "tin men," who were allowed to make and sell items from scraps of tin.

Meat and milk were part of the rations issued to station hands on all country properties. There was always meat for breakfast and for the main meal of the day. Sheep and cattle thrived in the upper Hunter Valley, and station owners and their men would kill sheep in the summer and cattle in the winter. As there was no refrigeration, most of the beef was preserved by being salted down in brine. Poultry was a luxury that was cooked only on Sundays. Even the Christmas turkey was boiled.

Milk was brought to the kitchen by the "cowboy." In the kitchen, the cook ladled her day's requirement from the bucket into jugs, pouring the rest into a large shallow bowl where it was left undisturbed to allow the cream to rise to the top. Next morning it was skimmed off to be made into butter in the wooden butter churn. To keep the butter cool, the cook had to lower it into the nearby well.

The upper Hunter climate and the busy life of the cook on a large property did not allow for cosy chats in the kitchen; but when she had finished preparing the meat and vegetables the cook carried her large teapot along the narrow passageway to the adjacent room and joined the men for a discussion of the day's events. It was at this time that she relayed her mistress's orders for the meat and vegetables that were to be brought to the kitchen next morning. In the hot summer months the cook and the men sat on the sheltered verandah where the canvas water bags were hung in the shade. Despite the weather, the mistress of the house preferred her afternoon tea to be served, in the English tradition, in her sitting room. The cook took off her working apron and changed into her

Well-worn saddlebags used by the station-hands and the boss. The station brand was stamped on each bag; in addition, the master's bag bore a personal brand. The squat bag contained the quart-pot, essential to tea making.

The wall oven at Belltrees is lined with sandstock bricks made on the property; the table is made of ironbark, one of the most unyielding and durable of timbers. The stove rake was used to drag the ashes over the coals. Dampers or loaves of bread were placed into and removed from the oven on a wooden pallet. The derivation of the word "damper" is open to speculation. It may be a contraction of the name of a seaman, William Dampier, who landed in north-west Australia in 1688 and found little to eat. It is said that his cook rustled up a flour-and-water cake to remedy the situation. Or perhaps damper refers to the practice of damping down the campfire at night by smothering the glowing embers with ash. Deprived of oxygen, the coals continue to glow and can be rekindled quickly in the morning.

Shelving made from packing cases (above)—just one of the many examples of ingenuity through sheer necessity that characterized bush furniture. Many discarded items were pressed into service; kerosene tins and fruit boxes, for example, became tables and cupboards.

afternoon apron to carry the tray, bearing the silver teapot and English bone china cups, into the privacy of the main homestead.

During the summer months, the cook walked with her mistress to the nearby orchard to examine the ripening of the fruit and decide when they should begin their joint task of preserving it. The two women worked together in the cook's domain, bottling or preserving the fruit that was to be used throughout the year as puddings or in sweets—or in the chutneys, pickles, and jams that enhanced the simple homestead meals. The preserving and bottling of fruit was a ritual with the White family women. It is recorded in the station diaries that they even declined invitations to visit relatives who lived in cooler climates—and so avoid the summer heat—on the grounds that "they were too busy with their preserves."

The original orchard on Belltrees, 50 yards (45 meters) to the east of the cook's room, was set in half an acre (a fifth of a hectare) of alluvial land. In the temperate climate a variety of fruit and nuts was grown: apples, oranges, plums, apricots, nectarines, grapefruit, table grapes, mandarines, almonds, and walnuts. The cook also had a generous choice of vegetables, grown nearby on the same alluvial flats. Each day, a station-hand or garden boy brought a supply of vegetables or basketfuls of fruit to the cook's room. The station-hands did not mind this task, as they too shared in the produce from the orchard and vegetable garden.

The present Belltrees homestead was built in 1906. It is Edwardian in style, and much bigger and grander than the original colonial house and cook's room of 1836. The earlier building remains in its original state as a museum, and the Belltrees library contains valuable reference material about pioneering life. The station diaries and letter books tell us, for example, how the Aborigines would descend from the hills and eat the succulent watermelons that grew on the river flats, and how the Murrawin tribe found sheep easier to hunt and tastier to eat than the native animals.

The cook's room and its adjoining annex contain numerous examples of bush crafts and imported kitchen utensils. The timber shelves were made from packing cases in which goods arrived from overseas; later came gadgets from America, such as apple corers, that made the cook's work easier. The long-handled iron pots on the stove bear the stamp of A. Kenrick and Sons of West Bromwich, England. Candles, reminders of the many that were made from mutton tallow, can still be seen there. So too can the Little Dorrit stove that was used to heat the flat irons with which the cook pressed the large white damask tablecloths when her other duties were finished.

In 1991 the White family celebrated 160 years of their involvement with Belltrees. Six generations of the family have worked on the same land and cared for their farm workers, their stock, and the many rural buildings on the estate. In a pageant, staged to depict the history of Belltrees, the cook's room was remembered for the important part it played in the life and development of this pioneer settler's home.

The table is made of local hardwood. The silverware and bone china lend an air of gentility to their simple surroundings (opposite). Despite the isolation of the Australian bush, station owners maintained and treasured the traditions and refinement of their English origins.

THE CONTRIBUTORS

ANNEKE AMMERLAAN began her career as a trainee with the Dutch magazine *Libelle* and was later involved in the development of the first Dutch food magazine, *Tip,* to which she contributed articles and recipes. With this experience, she became a freelance writer and consultant, contributing to magazines and publishing eight cookbooks. She is now responsible for the food sections of the magazines *Nouveau* and *Man,* and acts as a culinary consultant to supermarkets and food producers.

GERTRUD BENKER is an editor and writer. She was born and educated in Germany, and has worked as a teacher and in publishing houses. For fourteen years she has been editor in chief of the periodical *Volkskunst.* She has written many articles and about fifteen books dealing with aspects of cultural history, including *In Alten Kuchen* (*In Old Kitchens*) and *Bürgerliches Wohnen* (*Burgers' Housing*).

ANTONIO CARLUCCIO grew up in northern Italy and at an early age began his lifelong devotion to fungi. After moving to Vienna to study languages, he missed the traditional foods of his home and learned to cook. After twelve years as a wine merchant in Germany, he moved to England where he ran the Neal Street Restaurant, which he now owns. His first book, *An Invitation to Italian Cooking,* won the Bejam Cookery Book of the Year award, and his most recent, *A Passion for Mushrooms,* has been translated into five languages. He is a regular broadcaster on television about Italian, and especially mushroom, cooking.

SHIRLEY COLLINS was born in Texas, on the Mexican border, where she was beguiled by the sights, smells, and sounds of the local markets. She began cooking as a child, moved to Seattle, and in 1972 opened a store for cooks in the Pike Place Farmers' Market, where she was able to meet and cook for many famous cooks, and to find a niche in the international community of food lovers. She considers herself fortunate to live in a place so blessed with varied fresh food. She has studied at the Dieppe School of Cooking in France and with several international chefs, and writes a regular column in Seattle *Home and Garden* magazine.

SIR TERENCE CONRAN began his diverse career as a textile designer in London. He soon branched out into industrial design and in 1956 established the Conran Design Group, one of the largest design organizations in Europe. In 1964 he opened the first Habitat store, and in 1990 retired as chairman of the huge retailing group Storehouse PLC. His encouragement of good design in the home and environment has been honored by many awards, including a knighthood in 1983. He is the author of several books about design, including *The House Book* and *The Kitchen Book.*

ALAN DAVIDSON is internationally renowned as both author and publisher. His book *Mediterranean Seafood* is a classic, and he is currently compiling the *Oxford Companion to Food.* After a career in the diplomatic service, in 1979 he and his wife Jane joined forces with Elizabeth David, Jill Norman, and Richard Olney to found Prospect Books, publishing on all aspects of food, as well as a journal, *Petit Propos Culinaires.* He also inspired and organized, with Dr Theodore Zeldin, the Oxford Symposium on Food History, held annually since 1981. In addition to writing the introduction, he has advised on contents and contributors for this publication.

MARIE-NOËLE DENIS has been researching popular Alsatian culture since 1968, and has written widely on the subject. In addition to many articles, she has co-authored three books: *Alsace* in the series "Rural French Architecture" (1978), *Popular Tales of Alsace* (1979), and *Alsatian Tales* (1986). She is currently researching two further books: one on traditional furniture and the other on country culture. She is in charge of research at the Centre National de la Recherche Scientifique and deputy director of the Laboratoire de Sociologie de la Culture Européenne in Strasbourg.

GUNILLA ENGLUND took her degree at Uppsala University in Sweden, and established a career in museums, running courses, giving lectures, and setting up exhibitions. Her specialist subjects are the development of the home, changes in food customs, and the food industry in Sweden. At the Technical Museum in Stockholm, where she now works, she organizes "women's days" and "technical days" to discuss the implications of everyday technology and encourage schoolgirls to study technical subjects. She also writes and broadcasts about cultural history, and is a member of several professional societies.

M. F. K. FISHER is beloved as a "food writer", a label that summarizes but does not characterize her inimitable style or her books, among them *How to Cook a Wolf, Serve It Forth, Consider the Oyster*, and a translation of Brillat-Savarin's *Physiology of Taste*. Born in Michigan, she moved at the age of four to Whittier, California, where her family remained for the next forty-two years. Mary Frances Kennedy married in 1929 and went with her husband, Alfred Young Fisher, to study in France. She married twice more, first to Dillwyn Parrish and then to Donald Friede, with whom she had two children. Since her days in France and Switzerland during her daughters' education, she has lived in northern California, where she continues to write as she has done since her first publication in 1935.

WILLIE GRAHAM is an architectural historian with the Colonial Williamsburg Foundation, where he is responsible for the recording of early vernacular architecture, and closely involved in the research, design, and building of reconstructions. He has also undertaken historical and architectural research for a number of other restoration projects. He is a member of several professional associations and foundations, and has published a number of reports and papers relating to architectural conservation and restoration.

NEVIN HALICI is a food writer and teacher. Born and raised in Konya, Turkey, she moved to Ankara to study nutrition and cooking. During her career as a cooking teacher, she developed an interest in folklore and collected recipes and food traditions from Anatolia. Working as a chef, she has prepared menus from classic and folkloric cuisines and has prepared exhibitions about them. In 1979 she published *Traditional Dishes of Konya*, followed by *Dishes of the Aegean Region* (1981) and *Dishes of the Mediterranean Region* (1983). Her special interest in Turkish cooking is reflected in two publications: *Turkish Cookery* (1985) and *Nevin Halici's Turkish Cookbook* (1989). She is currently working on a book on Mevlevi dishes.

GERALDENE HOLT is an internationally acclaimed food writer who, after a successful career as a studio potter and teacher, began to write about food as a result of selling homemade cakes on a market stall in the West Country of England. She is an acknowledged authority on the food of France, and writes and broadcasts on growing and cooking food. Her latest book, *The Gourmet Garden* (1990), follows the considerable success of *Recipes from a French Herb Garden*. Her articles appear regularly in *Homes and Gardens* and *BBC Good Food* magazines, and her series "The Cook's Garden" is published in *Taste* magazine.

RICHARD HOSKING is Professor of English Language and Culture at Hiroshima Shudo University, Japan. After graduating in oriental studies at Cambridge University, he was for ten years Assistant Keeper of Oriental Manuscripts and Printed Books at the British Museum. During this time he developed an interest in oriental food and cooking, and traveled widely to further his knowledge. In the past eighteen years, as Professor at Hiroshima Shudo University, he has extended his interest and expertise in Japanese food culture.

PHILIP IDDISON was born and educated in Yorkshire, England. His degree in civil engineering led to work in several countries, where a latent interest in food and cultural life became a major spare-time interest as he collected and recorded local recipes and information about ingredients in Kuwait, Iraq, and Turkey. Two years' residence in Bangkok has enabled him to research a glossary of Thai food, delving into areas previously untapped by research in the English language.

MARIA JOHNSON was born in Bulgaria and graduated as a graphic designer from the Bulgarian Academy of Arts in Sofia. She has worked in Bulgarian and English publishing houses, but is now a full-time writer about Bulgarian food and cooking. She has contributed to a number of magazines and cookbooks, participated in the Oxford Symposium on Food History, and is currently completing a major work, *Balkan Food and Cooking*.

DIANA SOUTHWOOD KENNEDY was born in England and emigrated to Canada in 1953. Four years later she moved to Mexico and married Paul P. Kennedy, a *New York Times* foreign correspondent. After his death, while retaining a teaching base in the United States, she built an ecological house in the state of Michoacan in Mexico where she does her research and writing. She has published many food articles and five books: *The Cuisines of Mexico* (1972), *The Tortilla Book* (1975), *Recipes from the Regional Cooks of Mexico* (1978), *Nothing Fancy* (1984), and *The Art of Mexican Cooking* (1989). She has been honored by the Mexican government with the Order of the Aztec Eagle.

GERALD LONG is a British journalist and communications consultant. For the past six years he has lived in France, moving between an apartment in Paris and an old farmhouse on the edge of Bayeux in Normandy. With a Cambridge degree in modern languages, he joined Reuters in 1948 and served from 1950 to 1960 as a foreign correspondent in France, Germany, and Turkey. From 1963 to 1981 he was chief executive of Reuters, and from 1981 to 1984 worked for Rupert Murdoch after his takeover of Times Newspapers. He is now based in Paris and pursues personal interests in Europe.

ELISABETH LUARD is a botanical and wildlife painter, and began her career as a food writer as a weekly columnist for *The Field*. A lifelong student of the history of cooking through living in different countries, she has an intimate knowledge of the cuisine and regional specialties of France, Spain, and Italy. Her first book, *The Country House Cookery Book*, was published in 1985, and later titles include *European Peasant Cookery, European Festival Food, The Barricaded Larder*, and a book of essays, *The Princess and the Pheasant*. She is joint cooking editor of *Country Living* magazine, writes a column for the *Scotsman* newspaper, and is currently filming a thirteen-part television series based on European peasant cooking.

ELISABETH LAMBERT ORTIZ is the author of a number of acclaimed books on ethnic cuisines. Born in London, she is married to Mexican Cesar Ortiz-Tinoco, a retired United Nations official, and has lived and worked in several countries. She is keenly interested in the origins of food, and has been called both a culinary archeologist and a culinary historian, though she prefers the simpler designation of food writer. Among her publications are books on Mexican, Caribbean, Japanese, Latin American, Spanish, and Portuguese cooking, and on British and French chefs.

SRI OWEN was born in central Sumatra, where both her parents were teachers. During the Second World War the family moved to Java, where she was educated. As a young lecturer, she met and married her English husband, and moved to London in the 1960s. She broadcast for the BBC Indonesian service, and simultaneously found that her Indonesian cooking was appreciated by friends. In 1976 her first book, *The Home Book of Indonesian Cookery*, was published, followed in 1980 by *Indonesian Food and Cookery*. From 1984 to 1987 she ran a shop selling Southeast Asian food, spices, and ingredients. She now writes full-time: her third book, *Indonesian and Thai Cookery*, was published in 1988 and several more are in preparation.

ALICIA RIOS was born in Madrid and studied philosophy and psychology at Madrid University. After twelve years lecturing in the history of psychology, she established and cooked for a restaurant in Madrid. Since 1986 she has been researching the history of food and cooking, with particular emphasis on Mediterranean cuisine and olive oil. She has traveled extensively giving talks and demonstrations on the use of olive oil, and teaching in cookery schools. She is a regular participant at the Oxford Symposium on Food History, co-author of *El Libro del Aceite y la Aceituna*, and contributor to a number of gastronomic magazines.

ROSEMARY RUDDLE was raised in a rural community in England, and trained and worked as a feature writer in London. After two years of living among the vineyards and winemakers of Burgundy, she began to specialize in writing about food. She has a particular interest in regional food and customs, and has owned a house in the Haute Savoie region of France since 1985.

JULIE SAHNI is a noted cookbook author and food journalist. Her *Classic Indian Cooking* was commended by the André Simon award committee in 1987, and *Classic Indian Vegetarian and Grain Cooking* won the Glenfiddich award for the best cookbook of 1987. She was the executive chef of two Indian restaurants and proprietor of Julie Sahni's Indian Cooking School in New York. She serves on the faculties of Boston University and New York University and is a regular contributor to the *New York Times*. She is a member of many professional food organizations, and continues to travel extensively throughout India.

RENA SALAMAN was born and raised in Athens. Married to an English academic, she now lives in London with her twin daughters. She has written several books on Greek and Mediterranean food, including *Greek Food, Mediterranean Vegetable Cooking, The Cooking of Greece and Turkey*, and *Greek Island Cookery*. She has also contributed articles on food and travel to a range of magazines and newspapers, and has appeared on radio and television programs about food and cooking.

FULVIA SESANI runs a cooking school in her Venetian palazzo, and travels widely to conduct courses in Venetian and international

cuisine. She has been called a "gastronomic engineer," and creates edible works of art in which the principles of design, taste, texture, and color are combined to create a perfectly balanced dish.

MARÍA JOSÉ SEVILLA-TAYLOR began her career as a wine specialist, and holds the prestigious Wine Diploma. Several years ago she turned her attention to food, and helped to set up the Information Department of the Spanish Promotions Centre in London. She is committed to the teaching of Mediterranean food so that the much-underestimated Spanish cuisine gains the recognition it deserves. Her book *Life and Food in the Basque Country* was published in 1989 and she is currently working on a new book about the traditional food of Andalusia.

R. E. F. SMITH is a Fellow of the Institute for Advanced Research in the Humanities at the University of Birmingham, England. Between 1967 and 1987 he was Professor of Russian at the University of Birmingham, with particular interest in the history of farming in Russia from prehistoric to modern times. He is the author of "The Russian State" in *Oxford Slavonic Papers* (1985) and, with David Christian, of *Bread and Salt: A Social and Economic History of Food and Drink in Russia* (1984).

ANITA STEWART is the author of five books about Canadian cooking, including *The Country Inns Cookbook* (1987), a Book of the Month Club selection. She contributes to a number of Canadian and international publications, and writes a weekly syndicated newspaper column. She is the Canadian writer for *Corporate and Incentive Travel Magazine*, and is on the advisory council for the Professional Association of Independent Innkeepers. A self-styled "nationalistic foodie," she continues to research Canadian food, its history and future, and is determined to seek out Canada's best and present it to the world.

JILL TILSLEY-BENHAM is a freelance writer and consultant who, having left an early career in theater and art, has devoted much of the past quarter century to a study of Islamic food history. She has published numerous papers on this subject for symposia in Oxford and Istanbul, and writes extensively on Middle Eastern culture and food, and travel throughout the world. She is currently writing a novel with an oriental–British background and is compiling a literary history of Islamic food.

CLIO WHITTAKER took her degree in Chinese at the School of Oriental and African Studies, London University. She spent a year at Beijing University (1978–79) and then managed the British Steel office there. After returning to England she worked for the British Council for five years, and now combines looking after two young children with writing and editing on a freelance basis.

JUDY WHITE is the mother of five sons and two daughters. She lives with her husband, Michael White, at Belltrees, near Scone, in New South Wales, Australia. She holds a Bachelor of Economics degree from the University of Sydney and a Master of Letters degree from the University of New England, and was awarded a Master of Arts (Honoris Causa) from the University of Newcastle. She was the recipient of a Women '88 Award for services to the Australian Bicentenary, and serves on several cultural and artistic committees. She has written and published several local histories, a history of land settlement in the Belltrees region, and photographic surveys of urban and rural life, and is currently working on a book about bush photography.

INDEX

❖

CREDITS

❖

PICTURES: BACK COVER *clockwise from top left* J. P. Bonhommet, Guy Bouchet, Robert Harding Picture Library, Elizabeth Whiting & Associates; **endpapers** Leo Meier/Weldon Trannies

1 Fritz von der Schulenburg; **2** Pierre Hussenot/Agence Top; **3** Pierre Hussenot/Agence Top; **4–5** Tosiaki Tanji/Tanji Co. Photo Library; **6** Fritz von der Schulenburg; **8** Guy Bouchet; **10** Pascal Chevallier/Agence Top; **11** Pascal Chevallier/Agence Top; **13** Gilles Guerin/Agence Top; **14–15** J. P. Bonhommet; **16** Spike Powell/Elizabeth Whiting & Associates; **17** Fritz von der Schulenburg/design A. De Montal; **18** Shona Wood (2); **19** *above* P. Rauter/Weidenfeld & Nicolson Ltd, *below* Ianthe Ruthven; **20** Fritz von der Schulenburg; **21** Shona Wood (2); **22** Guy Bouchet; **23** A. Chadefaux/Agence Top; **24** *above left, below left, above center, below center and above right* Guy Bouchet, *below right* Jacques Guillard/Scope; **25** Guy Bouchet; **26** Guy Bouchet; **27** Guy Bouchet; **28** Guy Bouchet; **29** Guy Bouchet; **30** Collection Goltziusmuseum, Venlo, the Netherlands; **31** Anneke Ammerlaan; **32** Spaarnestad Fotoarchief, Haarlem; **33** Spaarnestad Fotoarchief, Haarlem; **34** Collection Goltziusmuseum, Venlo, the Netherlands; **35** Anneke Ammerlaan; **36** Andrew Paine/Elizabeth Whiting & Associates (2); **37** Andrew Paine/Elizabeth Whiting & Associates; **38** World Press Network; **39** Fritz von der Schulenburg/design Sukie Schellenberg; **40** World Press Network; **41** Fritz von der Schulenburg/design Sukie Schellenberg; **42** Jacques Guillard/Scope; **43** Pierre Hussenot/Agence Top; **44–5** Musée de la Ville de Strasbourg; **46** *left* D. Czap/Agence Top, *right* Pierre Hussenot/Agence Top; **47** Pierre Hussenot/Agence Top; **48–9** Fritz von der Schulenburg; **50** Sofia Press Agency; **51** Sofia Press Agency; **52** Sofia Press Agency; **53** Sofia Press Agency; **54** Sofia Press Agency; **55** Sofia Press Agency (6); **56** Sofia Press Agency; **57** Tim Sharman (2); **58** Lars Hallén Design Press; **59** Lars Hallén Design Press; **60–1** Peter Solness/Wildlight; **62** Peter Solness/Wildlight; **63** Peter Solness/Wildlight; **64** *above* Christer Hallgren/Korthuset, *below* Lars Johansson/Korthuset; **65** G. Englund; **66** G. Englund; **67** G. Englund (2); **68–9** G. Englund; **70** Lars Hallén Design Press; **71** Lars Hallén Design Press (2); **72** Camera Press; **73** Camera Press; **74** Lala Aufsberg; **75** Gertrud Benker/Garten und Landschaft; **76** *above* Gertrud Benker/Bavaria, *below* Dr Bahnmüller/Bavaria; **77** Dr Bahnmüller/Bavaria; **78** Jacques Sierpinski/Scope (2); **79** André Fournier/Scope; **80** Mazin/Agence Top; **81** Pierre Putelat/Agence Top; **82** Jacques Guillard/Scope; **83** Jean-Daniel Sudres/Scope (2); **84–5** Helen Stylianou; **86** A. Pradera/Weldon Russell (2); **87** A. Pradera/Weldon Russell; **88** A. Pradera/Weldon Russell; **89** A. Pradera/Weldon Russell (3); **90** A. Pradera/Weldon Russell; **91** A. Pradera/Weldon Russell (2); **92** Jacques Guillard/Scope; **93** Pierre Hussenot/Agence Top; **94** Simon Brown/Conran Octopus Ltd; **95** Simon Brown/Conran Octopus Ltd; **96** Jacques Guillard/Scope; **97** Guy Bouchet (2); **98** *above* Michael Newton, *below* Guy Bouchet; **99** Guy Bouchet; **100** Guy Bouchet; **101** Guy Bouchet (2); **102** Michael Newton; **103** Guy Bouchet; **104** Jorge Lain/Weldon Russell; **105** Jorge Lain/Weldon Russell; **106** Jorge Lain/Weldon Russell (2); **107** Jorge Lain/Weldon Russell; **108** Jorge Lain/Weldon Russell; **109** Jorge Lain/Weldon Russell (4); **110** Guy Bouchet; **111** Guy Bouchet; **112** Guy Bouchet (2); **113** Guy Bouchet; **114** from *Greek Style* by Stafford Cliff & Suzanne Slesin/photography Gilles de Chabaneix (2); **115** Alex Dufort/Impact Photos; **116** from *Greek Style* by Stafford Cliff & Suzanne Slesin/photography Gilles de Chabaneix; **117** from *Greek Style* by Stafford Cliff & Suzanne Slesin/photography Gilles de Chabaneix; **118** from *Greek Style* by Stafford Cliff & Suzanne Slesin/photography Gilles de Chabaneix; **119** from *Greek Style* by Stafford Cliff & Suzanne Slesin/photography Gilles de Chabaneix; **120** Helen Stylianou; **121** Helen Stylianou; **122–3** Ianthe Ruthven; **124** Tim Street-Porter/Elizabeth Whiting & Associates; **125** Tim Street-Porter/Elizabeth Whiting & Associates; **126** *above left* John Wright/Hutchison Library, *below left, above center, below center, above right and below right* Michael Calderwood; **127** Tim Street-Porter/Elizabeth Whiting & Associates; **128** Tim Street-Porter/Elizabeth Whiting & Associates; **129** Tim Street-Porter/Elizabeth Whiting & Associates; **130** Michael Calderwood (2); **131** Michael Calderwood (3); **132** Paul Rocheleau; **133** Paul Rocheleau; **134** Paul Rocheleau (2); **135** Paul Rocheleau; **136** Willie Graham (2); **137** Willie Graham; **138** Willie Graham (2); **139** Paul Rocheleau; **140** Oregon Historical Society CN 021461; **141** Laurie Black; **142** Oregon Historical Society 03256075; **143** Oregon Historical Society (*above* CN018042, *below* CN021256); **144–5** Laurie Black; **147** Laurie Black; **148** Anita Stewart; **149** Anita Stewart; **150** Anita Stewart; **151** *left* Jim Merrithew, *right* Anita Stewart; **152** R. R. Swallows/Ontario Ministry of Agriculture & Food, Ontario Agricultural Museum Library/Archives (2); **153** National Archives of Canada; **154** Fritz von der Schulenburg; **155** Eric Hayes; **156** APL/Jessie Walker; **157** APL/Jessie Walker; **159** APL/Jessie Walker; **160** Security Pacific Historical Photographic Collection/Los Angeles Public Library; **161** Security Pacific Historical Photographic Collection/Los Angeles Public Library; **162** Tony Morrison/South American Pictures; **163** Carlos Reyes/Andes Press Agency; **164** Tony Morrison/South American Pictures; **165** Christo Reid/Stockshots; **166** *above* Christo Reid/Stockshots, *below* Robert Harding Picture Library; **167** Tony Morrison/South American Pictures; **168–9** Bob King/Stockshots; **170** Michelle Garrett/Insight (2); **171** Michelle Garrett/Insight; **172** Michelle Garrett/Insight (3); **173** Michelle Garrett/Insight (2); **174** Michelle Garrett/Insight (2); **175** Michelle Garrett/Insight; **176** Nevin Halici/Weldon Russell; **177** Jeremy Horner/Hutchison Library; **178** Nevin Halici/Weldon Russell (2); **179** Nevin Halici/Weldon Russell (2); **180** Nevin Halici/Weldon Russell; **181** *above* Robert Harding Picture Library, *below* Christina Dodwell/Hutchison Library; **182–3** Leo Meier/Weldon Trannies; **184** from *Indian Style* by Stafford Cliff & Suzanne Slesin/photography David Brittain (2); **185** from *Indian Style* by Stafford Cliff & Suzanne Slesin/photography David Brittain; **186** from *Indian Style* by Stafford Cliff & Suzanne Slesin/photography David Brittain; **187** Robbi Newman/Image Bank; **188** from *Indian Style* by Stafford Cliff & Suzanne Slesin/photography David Brittain; **189** from *Indian Style* by Stafford Cliff & Suzanne Slesin/photography David Brittain (2); **190** Robert Harding Picture Library; **191** Michael Freeman; **192** Nancy Durrell McKenna/Hutchison Library; **193** Robert Harding Picture Library (2); **194–5** Nancy Durrell McKenna/Hutchison Library; **196** Hiroaki Misawa; **197** Sekai Bunka Photo; **198** Hiroaki Misawa (2); **199** Sekai Bunka Photo; **200** Richard Hosking (5); **201** Robert Harding Picture Library; **202** Hiroaki Misawa; **203** Tosiaki Tanji/Tanji Co. Photo Library; **204** Michael Freeman; **205** Michael Freeman; **206** Michael Freeman (2); **207** Photobank; **208–9** Michael Freeman; **210** Photobank; **211** Photobank (5); **212** Leo Meier/Weldon Trannies; **213** Leo Meier/Weldon Trannies; **214** *above* Robert Harding Picture Library, *below* Pierette Collomb/Hutchison Library; **215** Leo Meier/Weldon Trannies; **216** *left* Robert Harding Picture Library; **216–17** Trevor Page/Hutchison Library; **218** Hutchison Library (2); **219** *above* Bruno Barbey/Magnum, *below* Christine Pemberton/Hutchison Library; **220** Tara Sosrowardoyo/Weldon Russell; **221** Tara Sosrowardoyo/Weldon Russell; **222** *above* Tara Sosrowardoyo/Weldon Russell, *below* R. Ian Lloyd/Hutchison Library; **223** Tara Sosrowardoyo/Weldon Russell; **224** Tara Sosrowardoyo/Weldon Russell; **225** Anita Corbin/Impact Photos; **226** Jon Bader/Weldon Russell; **227** Jon Bader/Weldon Russell; **228–9** Jon Bader/Weldon Russell; **230** Jon Bader/Weldon Russell; **231** Jon Bader/Weldon Russell (2); **232** Jon Bader/Weldon Russell; **233** Jon Bader/Weldon Russell; **234** Hutchison Library; **235** Fritz von der Schulenburg